MEISTER ECKHART

MEISTER ECKHART

Selections from His Essential Writings

Foreword by John O'Donohue

Edited by Emilie Griffin

Translation by Edmund Colledge, O.S.A.,

and Bernard McGinn

HarperOne

An Imprint of HarperCollins*Publishers*

HarperOne

MEISTER ECKHART: *Selections from His Essential Writings*. Original translation published by Paulist Press, 997 Macarthur Boulevard, Mahwah, NJ 07430; www.paulistpress.com. Copyright © 1981 by Paulist Press, Inc. Foreword © 2005 by John O'Donohue. All rights reserved. Printed in the United States of America. No part of this book may be used or reproduced in any manner whatsoever without written permission except in the case of brief quotations embodied in critical articles and reviews. For information address HarperCollins Publishers, 10 East 53rd Street, New York, NY 10022.

HarperCollins books may be purchased for educational, business, or sales promotional use. For information please write: Special Markets Department, HarperCollins Publishers, 10 East 53rd Street, New York, NY 10022.

HarperCollins Web site: http://www.harpercollins.com
HarperCollins®, ♠®, and HarperOne™ are trademarks of HarperCollins Publishers.

FIRST HARPERCOLLINS PAPERBACK EDITION PUBLISHED IN 1957

Library of Congress Cataloging-in-Publication Data
Eckhart, Meister, d. 1327
   [Selections. English. 2005]
   Meister Eckhart : selections from his essential writings / edited by Emilie Griffin ;
foreword by John O'Donohue ; translation by Edmund Colledge and Bernard McGinn.
     p. cm.
   ISBN 978–0–06–075065–7
   1. Mysticism—Early works to 1800. 2. Catholic Church—Sermons—Early works to 1800. 3. Sermons, German—Translations into English. 4. Sermons, Latin—Translations into English. I. Title
BV5080.E3213   2005
248—dc22   2004059676

09 10 11 12 13 RRD(H) 10 9 8 7 6 5 4 3

CONTENTS

Foreword by John O'Donohue vii

Counsels on Discernment 1

Selected Sermons 63

On Detachment 103

The Book of Divine Consolation,
    from The Book of "Benedictus" 119

FOREWORD

Frequently, it takes us longest to arrive at what is nearest. Thought itself is one of the great mysteries. We engage in it in every moment, yet we are seldom aware of the distance we travel and the depth to which we travel in even the simplest act of thought. A great philosopher is a poet of thought. In his hands, thoughts shine like diamonds illuminating the dark memory and gestation of the earth and capturing the longing of eternal light. Indeed, thoughts become mirrors in which we gain fugitive glimpses of who we are and where our destination lies. Thoughts are the crevices where the vast silence of Being is voiced. In an archaic sense, to think is to participate in the mind of God.

Meister Eckhart is one of the great poets of thought. After seven hundred years, we can still enter the cathedral of thought that he built. There we will experience the haunting light, color, and tenderness of what he shows; we will be challenged to the roots of our souls by the fierceness, opaqueness, and danger of God. In Eckhart, the soul is the central threshold. It holds together the symphony of symmetries that play throughout all his explorations. Eckhart says that the soul has two faces: one that is permanently turned toward God, and another that always faces the world. The creative and critical negotiation of the tension between these two faces is the secret force that animates all his thinking. The soul is our door into the divine. In an age that has reduced identity to biography, Eckhart reminds us that identity is a more sublime and eternal presence. He says that there is a dimension of the soul that neither time nor flesh nor any created thing can touch. In one of his sermons—not included in this collection—he says: "The soul is created as if at a point between time and eternity, which touches both. With the higher powers she touches eternity, but with the lower powers she touches time. She works in time not according to it but according to eternity." Always in Eckhart, we are reminded of the call and duty we have to our eternal inheritance. We are the custodians of infinite thresholds.

Spirituality nowadays is weighted down with a vast panoply of methodologies and pathways. Into the clutter of this spiritual industry the clarity of Meister Eckhart shines like a light that relieves and refreshes. In contrast to many of his contemporaries, he had no recourse to the notion of a spiritual journey or path. The divine is not a distant goal toward which one must perennially labor like some haunted Sisyphus. There is nothing nearer to us than the divine; we need only slip into rhythm with it. We are in fact already home—as he says, "in the house we have never left."

In some strange and utterly distinctive way, Eckhart managed to break through to the divine ground. Put extremely, it is as though Eckhart speaks from within God. It is this subversive viewing point that makes for the beautiful strain in his thought. No number of accumulated or innovative perspectives could throw the lineaments of the eternal into the relief that Eckhart achieves. This is the reason that his language is at once lyrical and speculative. He is not speaking *about* God; he is speaking *of* God.

Reading Eckhart is, then, akin to reading the Poem of God. In him form and content are one. His language is cut with finesse and precision that achieves for the individual reader unique experiential and speculative apertures into the divine presence. Consequently, the act of reading him is one in which the usual roles of subject and object become reversed; rather than simply reading a text, the reader soon has the strange experience of the text beginning to read the reader. The texts are utterly alive with a subtle, woven density that invites the reader to return to them again and again in order to further sound out their divine echo; this means inevitably that an initial acquaintance with Eckhart develops into a lifelong and life-altering adventure.

Meister Eckhart emerges at a point in the thirteenth century where fascinating pathways of thought converge. His vast erudition is a ferment of all the great philosophers who preceded him—among them Plato, Aristotle, Plotinus, Albertus Magnus, and Thomas Aquinas. Because his gaze was centered on something so distinctively different, his vision becomes the site where the thought of his predecessors is angled uniquely to portray what he glimpsed. His is no abstract theory; the speculative serves to intensify the lyrical access to Presence, and the lyrical in turn serves to ground experientially the huge sweep of the speculative. The unity of this two-dimensional reach is most evident in his writing "On Detachment." This is a relatively meager treatise, but it serves to outline the new region that he is mapping. This is a zone where all attachment and all perspectives heretofore melt in order for something totally other to become available. Detachment is absolute clearance for nothing other than God; it is a total state. Eckhart says: "Now, detachment approaches so closely to nothingness that there can be nothing between perfect detachment and nothingness." It is absolute and direct and beyond all particularity. This is the nature of God: "God has stood in unmoved detachment since eternity in such a way that nothing transient can move him." Poetically, he says: "True detachment is nothing other than for the spirit to stand as immovable against whatever may chance to it of joy and sorrow, honor, shame, and disgrace, as a mountain of lead stands before a little breath of wind."

Detachment serves the birth of God in the soul. This is the moment when the soul relinquishes the fragmentation of the world and slips in again to the seamlessness of the eternal. Eckhart states: "The soul brings forth in herself God out of God and into God; she bears him truly outside of herself. She does this by bearing God *there*, where she is Godlike; *there* she is an image of God." One could claim that for Eckhart the incarnation achieves full realization in the birth of God in the soul. This capacity to bring God to birth invests individuality with huge creativity; it is the deepest longing of the human heart.

Eckhart's thought-world is fascinating; indeed, he pushes thought to its furthest inner and outer frontiers. To enter this world is to undergo transformation. Eckhart's crystal thought-shapes continue to linger in one's mind; somehow he becomes a true anchor for divine longing and a magnificent voyager to regions that one never imagined it possible to visit in thought.

—JOHN O'DONOHUE

COUNSELS ON
DISCERNMENT

These are the conversations that the vicar of Thuringia, the prior of Erfurt, Friar Eckhart of the order of Preachers, held with those young men who, conversing, asked him about many things as they sat with each other at Collation.

Counsel 1: About true obedience

True and perfect obedience is a virtue above all virtues, and no work is so great that it can be achieved or done without this virtue; and however little and however humble a work may be, it is done to greater profit in true obedience, be it saying Mass, hearing it, praying, contemplating, or whatever else you can think of. But take as humble a work as you like, whatever it may be: true obedience makes it finer and better for you. Obedience always produces the best of everything in everything. Truly, obedience never perturbs, never fails—whatever one is doing—in anything that comes from true obedience, for obedience neglects nothing that is good. Obedience need never be troubled, for it lacks no good thing.

When a man in obedience goes out of himself and renounces what he possesses, God must necessarily respond by going in there, for if anyone does not want something for himself, God must want it as if for himself. If I deny my own will, putting it in the hands of my superior, and want nothing for myself, then God must want it for me, and if he fails me in this matter, he will be failing himself. So in all things, when I do not want something for myself, God wants it for me. Now, pay good heed: what is it that God wants for me that I do not want for myself? When I empty myself of self, he must necessarily want everything for me that he wants for himself, neither more nor less, and in the same manner as he wants it for himself. And if he were not to do this, by that truth which is God, he would not be just, nor would he be the God that it is his nature to be.

In true obedience there should be no trace of "I want it so, or so," or "I want this or that," but there should be a pure going out from what is yours. And therefore in the best of all prayers that a man can pray, there should not be "Give me this virtue, or that way of life," or "Yes, Lord, give me yourself, or give me everlasting life," but "Lord, give me nothing but what you will, and do, Lord, whatever and however you will in every way." That is superior to the first way of praying as the heavens are above the earth. And when one has concluded that prayer, one has prayed well, for then one has in true obedience wholly entered into God. And, just as true obedience should have no "I want it so," so also one should not hear from obedience "I do not want," because "I do not want" is a sure poison for all obedience. That is what Saint Augustine says: "God's faithful servant has no desire for people to say or to give to him, or what he likes to hear or see, for his first and his greatest aim is to hear what is most pleasing to God."

Counsel 2: Of the most powerful prayer, and of the highest work of all

The most powerful prayer, and almost the strongest of all to obtain everything, and the most honorable of all works, is that which proceeds from an empty spirit. The emptier the spirit, the more is the prayer and the work mighty, worthy, profitable, praiseworthy, and perfect. The empty spirit can do everything.

What is an empty spirit?

An empty spirit is one that is confused by nothing, attached to nothing, has not attached its best to any fixed way of acting, and has no concern whatever in anything for its own gain, for it is all sunk deep down into God's dearest will and has forsaken its own. A man can never perform any work, however humble, without it gaining strength and power from this.

We ought to pray so powerfully that we should like to put our every member and strength, our two eyes and ears, mouth, heart, and all our senses to work; and we should not give up until we find that we wish to be one with him who is present to us and whom we entreat—namely, God.

Counsel 3: Of people who have not denied themselves and are full of their own will

People say: "O Lord, how much I wish that I stood as well with God, that I had as much devotion and peace in God as others have. I wish that it were so with me!" Or "I should like to be poor," or else "Things will never go right for me till I am in this place or that, or till I act one way or another. I must go and live in a strange land, or in a hermitage, or in a cloister."

In fact, this is all about yourself, and nothing else at all. This is just self-will, only you do not know it, or it does not seem so to you. There is never any trouble that starts in you that does not come from your own will, whether people see this or not. We can think what we like: that a man ought to shun one thing or pursue another—places and people and ways of life and environments and undertakings. That is not the trouble; such ways of life or such matters are not what impedes you. It is what you are in these things that causes the trouble, because in them you do not govern yourself as you should.

Therefore, make a start with yourself, and abandon yourself. Truly, if you do not begin by getting away from yourself, wherever you run to, you will find obstacles and trouble wherever it may be. People who seek peace in external things—be it in places or ways of life or people or activities or solitude or poverty or degradation—however great such a thing may be or whatever it may be, still it is all nothing and it gives no peace. People who seek in that way are doing it all wrong; the further they wander, the less will they find what they are seeking. They go around like someone who has lost his way; the farther he goes, the more lost he is. Then what ought he to do? He ought to begin by forsaking himself, because then he has forsaken everything. Truly, if a man renounced a kingdom or the whole world but held on to himself, he would not have renounced anything. What is more, if a man renounces himself, whatever else he retains, riches or honors or whatever it may be, he has forsaken everything.

About what Saint Peter said: "See, Lord, we have forsaken everything" (Mt 19:27)—and all that he had forsaken was just a net and his little boat—there is a saint who says: "If anyone willingly gives up something little, that is not all which he has given up, but he has forsaken everything that worldly men can gain and what they can even long for; for whoever has renounced his own will and himself has renounced everything, as truly as if he had possessed it as his own, to dispose of as he would." For what you choose not to long for, you have wholly forsaken and renounced for the love of God. That is why our Lord said: "Blessed are the poor in spirit" (Mt 5:3)—that is, in the will. And no one ought to be in doubt about this; if there were a better form of living, our Lord would have said so, as he also said: "Whoever wishes to come after me, let him deny himself" (Mt 16:24); as a beginning; everything depends on that. Take a look at yourself, and whenever you find yourself, deny yourself. That is the best of all.

Counsel 4: Of the profits of self-abandonment, which one should practice inwardly and outwardly

You should know that there was never any man in this life who forsook himself so much that he could not still find more in himself to forsake. There are few people who see this to be true and stick by it. This is indeed a fair exchange and an honest deal:

by as much as you go out in forsaking all things, by so much, neither less nor more, does God go in, with all that is his, as you entirely forsake everything that is yours. Undertake this, and let it cost you everything you can afford. There you will find true peace, and nowhere else.

People ought never to think too much about what they could do, but they ought to think about what they could be. If people and their way of life were only good, what they did might be a shining example. If you are just, then your works, too, are just. We ought not to think of building holiness upon action; we ought to build it upon a way of being, for it is not what we do that makes us holy, but we ought to make holy what we do. However holy the works may be, they do not, as works, make us at all holy; but, as we are holy and have being, to that extent we make all our works holy, be it eating, sleeping, keeping vigil, or whatever they may be. It does not matter what men may do whose being is mean; nothing will come of it. Take good heed: We ought to do everything we can to be good. It does not matter so much what we may do, or what kinds of works ours may be; what matters is the ground on which the works are built.

Counsel 5: See what can make our being and our ground good

A man's being and ground—from which his works derive their goodness—is good when his intention is wholly directed to God. Set all your care on that: that God become great within you, and that all your zeal and effort in everything you do and in everything you renounce be directed toward God. Truly, the more you do this in all your works, whatever they are, the better they are. Cleave to God, and he will endow you with all goodness. Seek God, and you will find God and every good thing as well. Yes, truly, with such an attitude you could tread upon a stone, and that would be a more godly thing for you to do than for you to receive the Body of our Lord, if then you were thinking more of yourself, with less detachment. If we cling to God, then God and all virtues cling to us. And what once you were seeking now seeks you; what once you hunted after now hunts you; and what you once wished to shun now avoids you. Therefore to him who clings greatly to God, everything clings that is godly, and from him everything takes flight that is unlike God and alien to him.

Counsel 6: Of detachment and of the possession of God

I was asked: "Since some people keep themselves much apart from others, and most of all like to be alone, and since it is in this and in being in church that they find peace, would that be the best thing to do?" Then I said: "No! And see why not!" If all is well with a man, then truly, wherever he may be, whomever he may be with, it is well with him. But if things are not right with him, then everywhere and with everybody it is all wrong with him. If it is well with him, truly he has God with him. But whoever really and truly has God, he has him everywhere: in the street and in company with everyone, just as much as in church or in solitary places or in his cell. But if a man really has God, and has only God, then no one can hinder him.

Why?

Because he has only God, and his intention is toward God alone, and all things become for him nothing but God. That man carries God in his every work and in every place, and it is God alone who performs all the man's works; for whoever causes the work, to him it belongs more properly and truly than it does to the one who performs it. Then let our intention be purely and only for God, and then truly he must perform all our works, and no person, no crowds, no places can hinder him in all his works. In the same way, no one can hinder this man, for he intends and seeks and takes delight in nothing but God, for God has become one with the man in all his intention. And so, just as no multiplicity can disturb God, nothing can disturb or fragment this man, for he is one in that One where all multiplicity is one and is one unmultiplicity.

A man should accept God in all things, and should accustom himself to having God present always in his disposition and his intention and his love. Take heed how you can have God as the object of your thoughts whether you are in church or in your cell. Preserve and carry with you that same disposition when you are in crowds and in uproar and in unlikeness. And, as I have said before, when one speaks of likeness, one does not mean that we should pay like attention to all works or all places or all people. That would be quite wrong, because praying is a better work than spinning, and the church is a better place than the street. But you ought in your works to have a like disposition and a like confidence and a like love for your God and a like seriousness. Believe me, if you were constant in this way, no one could come between you and the God who is present to you.

But a man in whom truly God is not but who must grasp God in this thing or in that from outside, and who seeks God in unlike ways, be it in works or people or places—such a man does not possess God. And it may easily be that something hinders such a man, for he does not possess God, and he does not seek him alone, nor does he love and intend him alone; and therefore it is not only bad company that hinders him. Good company can also hinder him—not just the street, but the church, too; not only evil words and deeds, but good words and deeds as well. For the hindrance is in him, because in him God has not become all things. Were that so, everything would be right and good for him, in every place and among all people, because he has God, and no one can take God away from him or hinder him in his work.

On what does this true possession of God depend, so that we may truly have him?

This true possession of God depends on the disposition, and on an inward directing of the reason and intention toward God—not on a constant contemplation in an unchanging manner; for it would be impossible for nature to preserve such an intention, and very laborious, and not the best thing, either. A man ought not to have a God who is just a product of his thought, nor should he be satisfied with that, because if the thought vanished, God, too, would vanish. But one ought to have a God who is present, a God who is far above the notions of men and of all created things. That God does not vanish if a man does not willfully turn away from him.

The man who has God essentially present to him grasps God divinely, and to him God shines in all things; for everything tastes to him of God, and God forms himself for the man out of all things. God always shines out in him. In him there is a detachment and a turning away, and a forming of his God whom he loves and who is present to him. It is like a man consumed with a real and burning thirst, who may well not drink and may turn his mind to other things. But whatever he may do, in whatever company he may be, whatever he may be intending or thinking of or working at, still the idea of drinking does not leave him, as long as he is thirsty. The more his thirst grows, the more the idea of drinking grows and intrudes and possesses him and will not leave him. Or if a man loves something ardently and with all his heart, so that nothing else has savor for him or touches his heart but that, and that and nothing but that is his whole object: truly, wherever he is, whomever he is with, whatever he may undertake, whatever he does, what he so loves never passes from his mind, and he finds the image of what he loves in everything, and it is the more present to him the more his love grows and grows. He does not seek rest, because no unrest hinders him.

Such a man finds far greater merit with God, because he grasps everything as divine and as greater than things in themselves are.

Truly, to this belong zeal and love and a clear apprehension of his own inwardness, and a lively, true, prudent, and real knowledge of what his disposition is concerned with amid things and persons. A man cannot learn this by running away, by shunning things and shutting himself up in an external solitude; rather, he must practice a solitude of the spirit wherever or with whomever he is. He must learn to break through things and to grasp his God in them and to form him in himself powerfully, in an essential manner. This is like someone who wants to learn to write: If he is to acquire the art, he must certainly practice it hard and long, however disagreeable and difficult this may be for him and however impossible it may seem. If he will practice it industriously and assiduously, he learns it and masters the art. To begin with, he must indeed memorize each single letter and get it firmly into his mind. Then, when he has the art, he will not need to think about and remember the letters' appearance; he can write effortlessly and easily—and it will be the same if he wants to play the fiddle or to learn any other skill. It will always be enough for him to make up his mind to do the hard work that the art demands; and even if he is not thinking about it all the time, still, whatever he may be thinking when he does perform it, this will be from the art he has learned.

So a man must be penetrated with the divine presence, and be shaped through and through with the shape of the God he loves, and be present in him, so that God's presence may shine out to him without any effort. What is more, in all things let him acquire nakedness, and let him always remain free of things. But

at the beginning there must be attentiveness and a careful formation within himself, like a schoolboy setting himself to learn.

Counsel 7: How a man should perform his work in the most reasonable way

One often finds people who are not impeded by the things that
are around them—and this is easy to attain if one wishes—nor
do they have any constant thought about them. For if the heart is
full of God, created things can have and find no place in it. But,
what is more, this alone should not satisfy us. We ought to turn
everything into great profit, whatever it may be, wherever we
may be, whatever we see or hear, however strange or unlikely it
may be. Then for the first time all is well with us and not until
then, and one will never come to an end in this. One can always
go on increasing in this, gaining more and more from it in true
growth.

And in all his activities and under all circumstances a man
should take care to use his reason, and in everything he should
have a reasonable consciousness of himself and of his inwardness,
and find God in all things, in the highest degree that is possible.
For a man ought to be as our Lord said: "You should be like men
who are always watching and waiting for their master" (Lk
12:36). Truly, people who wait stay awake and look around them
for whence he for whom they are waiting may be coming; and
they are on the lookout for him in whatever may come, however
unknown it may be to them, for perhaps he might somehow be

in it. So we should have in all things a knowing perception of our master. We must show zeal in this, and it must cost us everything we are capable of in mind and body, and so it will be well with us, and we shall find God in everything alike, and find God always alike in all things.

Certainly, one work differs from another; but whoever undertakes all his works in the same frame of mind, then, truly, all that man's works are the same. Indeed, for the man for whom God shines forth as directly in worldly things as he does in divine things and to whom God would be so present—for such a man things would be well. Not indeed that the man himself would be doing worldly things, unlike to God; rather, whatever external matters he chanced to see and hear, he would refer it all back to God. Only he to whom God is present in everything and who employs his reason in the highest degree and has enjoyment in it knows anything of true peace and has a real kingdom of heaven.

For if things are to go well with a man, one of two things must always happen to him: either he must find and learn to possess God in works, or he must abandon all works. But since a man cannot in this life be without works, which are proper to humans and are of so many kinds, therefore he must learn to possess his God in all things and to remain unimpeded, whatever he may be doing, wherever he may be. And therefore if a man who is beginning must do something with other people, he ought first to make a powerful petition to God for his help, and put him immovably in his heart and unite all his intentions, thoughts, will, and power to God, so that nothing else than God can take shape in that man.

Counsel 8: Of constant zeal for the highest growth

A man should never be so satisfied with what he does or accomplish it in such a way that he becomes so independent or overconfident in his works that his reason becomes idle or lulled to sleep. He ought always to lift himself up by the two powers of reason and will, and in this to grasp at what is best of all for him in the highest degree, and outwardly and inwardly to guard prudently against everything that could harm him. So in all things he will lack nothing, but he will grow constantly and mightily.

Counsel 9: How the inclination to sin always helps a man

You must know that when vices attack us, this is never for the just man without great profit and utility. See carefully. There are two men, and one of them may be so disposed that shortcomings never or seldom touch him. But it is the other man's nature that they do; the outward presence of things so stirs the outer man in him that he is easily moved to anger or to vain ambition or it may be to bodily lusts, whatever the circumstance may be. But in his highest powers he always stands firm and unmoved, never willing to commit sin, not anger or any other, and he puts up great resistance against sin, because the sin is perhaps a weakness of his nature, as many men are naturally wrathful or proud or whatever it may be, and yet he does not want to sin. This man is far more to be praised, and his reward is much greater and his virtue is much more excellent than that of the first man, for the perfection of virtue comes from fighting; as Saint Paul says: "Virtue is made perfect in infirmity" (2 Cor 12:9).

The inclination to sin is not sin, but to want to sin is sin, to want to be angry is sin. Indeed, if a man thought rightly, and if he had the power to choose, he would not want to choose that his inclination to sin should die in him, because without it he would lack decision in everything and in all that he did he would be without care in these matters, and, too, he would lose the honor of the battle and of the victory and of the reward; for it is the assault and the force of vice that bring virtue and the reward for striving. It is this inclination that makes a man ever more zealous to exercise himself valiantly in virtue and impels him mightily toward virtue, and it is a stern whip driving a man on to caution and virtue. For the weaker a man finds himself, the more should he protect himself with strength and victory. For virtue and vice, too, are a question of the will.

Counsel 10: How the will can do all things, and how all virtues are a question of the will, if only it is just

A man should not be too afraid of anything as long as he sees that he has goodwill, nor should he be depressed if he cannot accomplish his will in his deeds; but he should not consider himself deprived of virtue if he finds in himself a will that is just and good, because the virtues and everything that is good are a question of goodwill. You can want for nothing if you have a true and just will—not love or humility or any virtue. But what you desire with all your might and all your will, that you have, and God and all created things cannot take it away from you if only your will is wholly just and godly and is directed toward the present. So do not say: "One day I should like . . . ," because that would be for the future, but "I want it to be so now." Pay good attention: if something is more than a thousand miles away and I want to have it, I really have it—more than what is lying in my lap and what I do not want.

What is good has not less power to draw toward good than what is evil has to draw toward evil. Pay heed: though I might never perform any evil deed, if I have the will to evil, I have the sin, as if I had performed the deeds; and I could commit as great sins only in my will as if I had murdered the whole human race, even if I had actually never done anything of the kind. So why should the same thing not be true of a good will? Truly, and far more so!

Indeed, with my will I can do everything: I can take upon myself every man's toil; I can feed every poor man; I can do every man's work and anything else that you could think of. If you are not lacking in will but only in power, in truth in God's sight you have done it all, and no one can take it away from you, or stop you for a moment from doing it; for wanting to do something as soon as I can and having done it are the same in the sight of God. What is more, if I wanted to have as great a will as the whole world has, and if my longing for that is great and complete, then indeed I have it; for what I want to have, I have. And, too, if I truly wanted to have as much love as all men have ever gained, or to praise God as much, or anything else you can think of, then, indeed, I have it all, if only your will is complete.

Now, you might ask, "When is the will a just will?"

The will is complete and just when it is without any self-seeking, and when it has forsaken itself and has been formed and shaped into God's will. And the more this is so with a man, the more is his will just and true. And in that will you can accomplish everything, be it love or whatever you want.

Now, you ask: "How could I have this love, while I do not feel it and am not aware of it, and yet I see many people who accomplish great deeds, and I see in them great devotion and marvelous qualities I do not have?"

Here you ought to observe two properties that love possesses: one is the being of love; the other is the deeds or the manifestation of love. The place where love has its being is only in the will; the man who has more will, he also has more love. But no one knows about anyone else, whether he has more of it; that lies hidden in the soul, as long as God lies hidden in the soul's ground. This love lies wholly in the will; whoever has more will, he also has more love.

Yet there is something else that is a manifestation and a deed of love. Often this appears plainly as inwardness and devotion and jubilation; and yet this is not always the best that could be. For it may be that it does not come from love; but perhaps it comes only from nature that a man experiences such savor and sweetness. It may be sent down from heaven, or it may be borne in from the senses. And those who have more of this are not always the best men; for even if such a gift be truly from God, our Lord often gives it to such people to entice and draw them on, and also to make them, through it, very withdrawn from others. Yet these same people, when later they have obtained more love, may then well not experience as much emotion and feeling, and from that it is well seen that they have love, if they cleave faithfully and steadily to God without such a prop.

And even if this really be love, it still is not the very best love. That can be seen when sometimes a man must abandon this kind of jubilation because of a better kind of love, and sometimes to perform a work of love, whether spiritual or bodily, when someone has need of him. I have said before: if a man was in an ecstasy, as Saint Paul was, and knew that some sick man needed him to give him a bit of soup, I should think it far better if he would abandon his ecstasy out of love and show greater love in caring for the other in his need.

Nor should a man think that in doing so he will be deprived of grace, for whatever he willingly abandons out of love will become a much greater reward for him; as Christ said: "Whoever has given up something for love of me, he will receive in return a hundred times as much" (Mt 19:29). Yes, truly, when a man forsakes something and denies it to himself for the love of God—yes, even if it be that a man has a great desire to experience such consolations and inwardness and does everything he can to obtain this and God does not give it to him, and he willingly relinquishes and forgoes this for God's love—then such a man will find in God what he seeks, just as if he had possessed as his own all the riches that ever were and had willingly relinquished, abandoned, and denied them for God's sake. He will receive a hundred times as much. For whatever a man would gladly have that he relinquishes and goes without for God's love, be it something material or spiritual, he will find all of it in God, just as if he had possessed it and had willingly abandoned it; for a man ought gladly to be robbed of all that he has for the love of God, and out of love he should wholly abandon and deny love's consolations.

That a man ought sometimes out of love to forgo such sensations Saint Paul in his love admonishes us when he says: "I have wished that I might be separated from Christ for the love of my brothers" (Rom 9:3). By that he means not the pure love of God, for from that he did not wish to be separated for one instant, not for the sake of everything that might be in heaven and on earth. He means the consolations of love.

But you must know that God's friends are never without consolation, for whatever God wills is for them the greatest consolation of all, whether it be consolation or desolation.

Counsel 11: What a man should do when God has hidden himself and he seeks for him in vain

You ought also to know that a man with goodwill can never lose God. Rather, it sometimes seems to his feelings that he loses him, and often he thinks that God has gone far away. What ought you to do then? Just what you did when you felt the greatest consolation. Learn to do the same when you are in the greatest sorrow, and under all circumstances behave as you did then. There is no advice so good as to find God where one has left him; so do now, when you cannot find him, as you were doing when you had him; and in that way you will find him. But a good will never loses or seeks in vain for God. Many people say: "We have a good will," but they do not have God's will. They want to have their will, and they want to teach our Lord that he should be doing this and that. That is not a good will. We ought to seek from God what is his very dearest will.

This is what God looks for in all things: that we surrender our will. When Saint Paul had done a lot of talking to our Lord, and our Lord had reasoned much with him, that produced nothing, until he surrendered his will and said: "Lord, what do you want me to do?" (Acts 9:6). Then our Lord showed him clearly what he ought to do. So, too, when the angel appeared to our Lady, nothing either she or he had to say would ever have made her the Mother of God, but as soon as she gave up her own will, at that moment she became a true mother of the everlasting Word and she conceived God immediately; he became her son by nature. Nor can anything make a true man except giving up his will. Truly, without giving up our own will in all things, we never accomplish anything in God's sight. But if it were to progress so far that we gave up the whole of our will and had the courage to renounce everything, external and internal, for the love of God, then we would have accomplished all things, and not until then.

We find few people, whether they know it or not, who would not like this to be so for them: to experience great things, to have this way of living and this treasure. But all this is nothing in them except self-will. You ought to surrender yourself wholly to God in all things, and then do not trouble yourself about what he may do with his own. There are thousands of people, dead and in heaven, who never truly and perfectly forsook their own wills. Only a perfect and true will could make one enter perfectly into God's will and be without a will of one's own; and whoever has more of this, he is more fully and more truly established in God. Yes, one Hail Mary said when a man has abandoned himself is more profitable than to read the Psalms a thousand times over without that. With that, one pace forward would be better than to walk across the sea without it.

The man who in this way had wholly gone out of himself with everything that he possessed would indeed be established wholly in God, so that if anyone wanted to move him, he would first have to move God. For he is wholly in God, and God is around him as my cap is around my head. If anyone wanted to seize hold of me, first he would have to seize hold of my coat. In the same way, if I want to drink, the drink must first pass over my tongue; in this way the drink gives its flavor. If the tongue is coated with bitterness, then truly, however sweet the wine itself may be, it must become bitter through the means by which it comes to me. In truth, if a man had completely abandoned everything that is his, he would be so surrounded by God that no created thing could move him unless it had first moved God. Whatever would reach him would first have to reach him by means of God. So it will find its savor from God, and will become godlike. However great a sorrow may be, if it comes by means of God, then God has suffered it first. Yes, by that truth which is God, however little a sorrow may be that comes upon a man, as he places it in God, be it some displeasure or contradiction, it moves God immeasurably more than the man; and if it is grievous for the man, it is more so for God. But God suffers it for the sake of some good thing that he has provided in it for you, and if you will suffer the sorrow that God suffers and that comes to you through him, it will easily become godlike: contempt, it may be, just as respect; bitterness just as sweetness; the greatest darkness just as the brightest light. It takes all its savor from God, and it becomes godlike, for it forms itself wholly in his image, whatever comes to this man, for this is all his intention and nothing else has savor for him; and in this he accepts God in all bitterness, just as in the greatest sweetness.

The light shines in darkness, and there man perceives it. What is the use to people of teaching or light unless they use it? If they are in darkness or sorrow, they ought to see the light.

Yes, the more that we possess ourselves, the less do we possess. The man who has gone out of what is his own could never fail to find God in anything he did. But if it happened that a man did or said something amiss, or engaged in matters that were wrong, then God, since he was in the undertaking at the beginning, must of necessity take this harm upon him, too; but you must under no circumstances abandon your undertaking because of this. We find an example of this in Saint Bernard and in many other saints. One can never in this life be wholly free from such mishaps. But because some weeds happen among the corn, one should not for that reason throw away the good corn. Indeed, if it were well with a man and he knew himself well with God, all such sorrows and mishaps would turn into his great profit. For to good men all things come to good, as Saint Paul says (Rom 8:28); and, as Saint Augustine says: "Yes, even sins."

Counsel 12: Of sins and of how we should act when we find ourselves in sin

Indeed, to have committed sins is not sin, if we have sorrow for them. A man should never wish to commit sin, not for anything that could be in time or in eternity—not mortal sins, not venial, not any sins at all. A man who knew himself well with God ought always to see that our faithful and loving God has brought man out of a sinful life into a life that is divine, and out of him who was his enemy God has made a friend, and that is more than to create a new earth. This would be one of the greatest reasons for a man to become wholly established in God; and it would be astonishing how greatly it would kindle the man to a stronger and greater love, so that he would wholly abandon what is his own.

Yes, that man would indeed be established in God's will who would not wish that the sin into which he had fallen had never been committed; not because it was against God but since, through that, you are obliged to greater love, and, through that, brought low and humbled. He should wish only that he had not acted against God. But you should indeed trust God, that he would not have inflicted this on you had he not wished to produce from it what is best for you. But when a man with all his resolution rises up from his sins and turns wholly away from them, our faithful God then acts as if he had never fallen into sin. For all his sins, God will not allow him for one moment to suffer. Were they as many as all men have ever committed, God will never allow him to suffer for this. With this man God can use all the simple tenderness that he has ever shown toward created beings. If he now finds the man ready to be different, he will have no regard for what he used to be. God is a God of the present. He takes and receives you as he finds you—not what you have been, but what you are now. All the harms and the insults that could come upon God for all sins he is gladly willing to suffer and to have suffered for many years so that a man thereafter may come to a greater knowledge of his love and so that man's love and gratitude may be so much greater and his zeal may be so much more ardent, which properly and frequently follows after our sins.

Therefore God gladly suffers the harm of sins, and has often suffered it, and most often he has permitted it to happen to men for whom he has provided that he would draw them to great things. Notice well: Who was dearer or closer to our Lord than were the apostles? But there was no one of them who did not fall into mortal sin; they had all been mortal sinners. In the Old Law and the New he often showed this through men who afterward were by far the dearest to him. And even now one seldom finds that people attain to anything good unless first they have gone somewhat astray. Our Lord's intention in this is that we should recognize his great mercifulness; and through it he wishes to exhort us to a greater and truer humility and devotion. For when repentance is renewed, so, too, love should be greatly increased and renewed.

Counsel 13: Of a twofold repentance

Repentance is of two kinds: one is of time and of the senses; the other is divine and supernatural. Repentance in time always declines into greater sorrow and plunges a man into lamentation, as if he must now despair; and there repentance remains in its sorrow, and can make no progress; nothing comes of it.

But divine repentance is quite different. As soon as a man has achieved self-loathing, at once he lifts himself up to God and establishes himself in an eternal turning away from all sin in an immovable will; and there he lifts himself up in great confidence to God and achieves a great security. And from this there comes a spiritual joy that lifts the soul up out of all sorrow and lamentation, and makes it secure in God. For the weaker a man finds himself and the more have been his misdeeds, the more cause he has to bind himself to God with an undivided love in which there is no sin or weakness. Therefore the best path up, which a man can proceed when he wants to go to God in all devotion, is for him to be sinless, made strong by a godly repentance.

And the heavier a man's sins are as he weighs them, the readier is God to forgive them, and to come to the soul, and to drive the sins out. Every man does his utmost to get rid of what most irks him. And the greater and the more the sins are, still immeasurably more is God glad and ready to forgive them, because they are irksome to him. And then, as godly repentance lifts itself up to God, sins vanish into God's abyss, faster than it takes me to shut my eyes, and so they become utterly nothing, as if they had never happened, if repentance is complete.

Counsel 14: Of true confidence and of hope

One ought to test whether love be true and perfect by asking if one has great hope and confidence in God, for there is nothing by which one can better see whether one's love is total than by trust. For if one man loves another greatly and completely, that causes him to have trust; for everything that we dare trust to be in God we find in him truly and a thousand times more. And so, since no man could ever love God too much, so also no man could ever trust him too much. Nothing that a man can do is as fitting as to have great trust in God. God never ceased to achieve great things through those who ever gained great confidence in him. He has truly shown to all men that this trusting comes from love; for not only does love have trust, it also has true knowledge and unshakable certainty.

Counsel 15: Of a twofold certainty of everlasting life

In this life we have a twofold knowledge of everlasting life. One knowledge is when God himself imparts it to a man or sends it to him through an angel or shows it through a special illumination; this happens seldom and to few people.

The second knowledge, which is incomparably better and more profitable and happens often to all who are perfect in their love, is when a man, through the love and the intimacy that exist between his God and him, trusts in him so fully and is so certain of him that he cannot doubt. What makes him so certain is that he loves God in all his creatures without any distinction. And even if all God's creatures were to deny him and abjure him— yes, if God himself were to deny him—he would not mistrust; for love cannot mistrust: love has trust in everything that is good. There is no need for one to say anything to the lover and to his beloved, for once the lover knows that his beloved loves him, he knows at once everything that is for his good and makes for his happiness. For however great your love for him may be, of this you are sure: his love for you is greater beyond measure, and his trust in you is incomparably more. For he is Trust himself; one should be sure of this with him, and they are all sure of it who love him.

This certainty is by far greater, more complete and true than is the first, and it cannot deceive. To be told it in words could deceive and could easily be a false light. But this certainty one receives in all the powers of the soul, and it cannot deceive those who truly love God; they doubt as little as a man doubts in God, because love drives out all fear. "Love has no fear," as Saint Paul says; and as it is also written: "Love covers a multitude of sins" (1 Ps 4:8). For when sins occur, there cannot be complete trust or love, for love completely covers sin over; love knows nothing about sin. It is not as if a man had not sinned, but that love wholly destroys and drives out sin as if it had never been. For all God's works are wholly perfect and superabundant, so that whomever he forgives, he forgives wholly and completely, and great sinners more gladly than the lesser ones; and this makes a perfect trust. I estimate this to be far and incomparably better than the first knowledge; and it brings a greater reward and is more true, for it is not hindered by sin or by anything else. For if God finds a man to be in such a state of love, he judges him just as lovingly, whether or not the man may have done something greatly amiss. But the man who receives greater forgiveness should love more; as Christ our Lord said: "To whom more is for-given, let him love more" (Lk 7:47).

Counsel 16: Of true penitence and a blessed life

Many people think that they ought to perform great exterior works, such as fasting, going barefoot, and such things as that, which are called *penitence*. But the true and very best of all peni-tence, which greatly improves men and raises them to the highest, is for a man to have a great and perfect aversion to everything in himself and in all creatures that is not wholly God and godly, and for him to have a great and perfect and complete conversion to his dear God in a love so unshakable that his devo-tion to God and his longing for him be great. The more you have of this in any work, the more you are justified; and as this grows and grows, so you have more and more true penitence, and this will the more blot out sin and even sin's punishment. Yes, you could in a short time with great resolution turn away from all sin with a true disgust for it, and with equal resolution betake your-self to God, so that even if you had committed all the sins that have ever been done since the days of Adam and will ever be done, all that would be completely forgiven you and its punish-ment remitted, so that if you were to die this moment you would come into the presence of God.

This is true penitence, and it comes, particularly and most per-fectly, from what our Lord Jesus Christ suffered so fruitfully in his perfect penitence. The more that a man forms himself in that, the more do all sins and the pains of sin fall away from him. And it ought to be a man's habit at all times and in all his works to form himself in the life and the works of our Lord Jesus Christ in everything he does and refrains from and suffers and experiences. And let him think constantly of him as our Lord thought of us.

This penitence is a complete lifting up of the mind away from all things into God, and whatever the works may be in which you have found and still find that you can most perfectly achieve this, do them with no constraint; and if you are impeded in this by any exterior work—whether it be fasting, keeping vigil, reading, or whatever else—give it up and do not be afraid that in this you may be forgoing any of your penitence, because God has no regard for what your works are, but for what your love and devotion and intention in the works are. Our works do not greatly matter to him, but only our intention in all our works, and that we love him alone in all things. For the man is far too greedy who is not satisfied with God. All your works will be rewarded in your God's knowledge of them, and that in them he was your intention; and always be content with that. And the more that your intention is directed wholly and simply toward him, the more truly will all your works atone for all your sins.

And you must also reflect that God was the general redeemer of all the world, and I owe him far more gratitude for that than if he had redeemed me alone. So, too, ought you to be a general redeemer of everything in you that you have spoiled with your sins; and, doing that, put your whole confidence in him, for with your sins you have spoiled everything there is in you: your heart, your intellect, your body, your soul, your powers, everything about you and in you—all of it is sick and spoiled. So take refuge in him in whom there is nothing lacking, but everything that is good, so that he may be the general redeemer of all your shortcomings both internal and external.

Counsel 17: How a man should preserve himself in peace, if he does not find himself severely tried as Christ and many saints were; and how he ought to follow God

People may become anxious and distressed because the lives of our Lord Jesus Christ and of the saints were so harsh and laborious, and a man may be able to perform little like this and may not feel himself forced to do so. Therefore, when people find themselves unequal to this, they think that they are far away from God, and that they cannot follow him. No one ought to think this. No man ought ever under any circumstances to think himself far away from God, not because of his sins or his weakness or anything else. If it should ever be that your great sins drive you so far off that you cannot think of yourself as being close to God, still think of him as being close to you. For a man does himself great harm in considering that God is far away from him; wherever a man may go, far or near, God never goes far off. He is always close at hand, and even if he cannot remain under your roof, still he goes no farther away than outside the door, where he stands.

And it is the same with the labor of following God. Take heed of how you ought to follow him. You ought to know and to have taken heed of what it is that God is requiring most of you; for not everyone is called to come along the same way to God, as Saint Paul says. So if you find that your shortest way does not consist of many external works and great labors or mortifications—which, to look at things simply, are not so very important unless a man is especially called to them by God and has the strength to perform them all without damage to his spiritual life—and if you find that you are not like this, keep quite calm and do not let yourself be too concerned about it.

But you may say: "If this is not so important, why have so many of our forebears, so many saints, practiced it?"

But consider: Our Lord gave them this manner of life, and he also gave them the strength to act like that, so that they could follow this way of life, and what they did was very pleasing to him, and it was in so doing that they were to achieve their very best. But God has not made man's salvation depend on any such particular way of life. What is peculiar to one way of life is not found in another; but it is God who has endowed all holy practices with the power of fulfillment, and it is denied to no good way of life. For one good thing is not in opposition to another. And from this people ought to learn that they are doing wrong if they see or hear that some good man is not following their way of life and they decide that what he is doing is useless. If they do not like what he does, immediately they shut their eyes to what is good in what he does and his intention in doing it. That is not right.

People should have regard to the true devotion that is to be found in men's practices, and they should not despise what anyone does. It is not possible for everyone to live alike, for all men to follow one single way of life, or for one man to adopt what everyone else or what some one other man may be doing.

So let every man keep to his own pious practices; let him mix in it any other practice, accepting into what he does everything that is good. To change from one to another makes for instability in one's piety and in one's intention. What one such practice could give you, you could also obtain from another, if they are both good and praiseworthy and have only God as their intention; everyone cannot follow one single way. And it is the same with imitating the mortifications of such saints. You may well admire and be pleased by practices you still are not required to imitate.

But now you may say: "Our Lord Jesus Christ always practiced what was the very best, and it is always he whom we should imitate."

That is very true. One ought indeed to imitate our Lord, but still not in everything he did. Our Lord, we are told, fasted for forty days. But no one ought to undertake to imitate this. Many of his works Christ performed with the intention that we should imitate him spiritually, not physically. And so we ought to do our best to be able to imitate him with our reason, for he values our love more than our works. Each of us ought in our own ways to imitate him.

"And how?"

Take good heed: in everything.

"How, and in what way?"

As I have often said: "I esteem a work of the reason far higher than a work of the body."

"And how?"

Christ fasted for forty days. Imitate him by considering what you are sure that you are most inclined and ready to do; apply yourself to this and observe yourself closely. It is often more profitable for you to refrain from these things than to go without any food. Similarly, it is sometimes harder for you to suppress one word than to keep completely silent. So it is harder at times for a man to endure one little word of contempt, which really is insignificant, when it would be easy for him to suffer a heavy blow to which he had steeled himself, and it is much harder for him to be alone in a crowd than in the desert, and it is often harder for him to abandon some little thing than a big one, harder for him to carry out a trifling enterprise than one that people would think much more important. Thus a man in his weakness can very well imitate our Lord, and he need never consider himself far off from him.

Counsel 18: The way for a man to make proper use of the delicate food and fine clothing and pleasant companions to which his natural disposition inclines him

You must not concern yourself about food or clothing by worrying if they seem too good for you, but train the ground of your being and your disposition to be far above all this; and nothing ought to move your disposition to delight or to love except God alone. It should be far above everything else.

Why?

Because a man's interior life would indeed be deficient if he needed outer garments to guide it for him; it is the interior that should guide the exterior, as far as that is in your power. But if something different comes your way, in the ground of your being you can be content that you are so disposed that even if at another time something else should be given to you, you would receive that just as willingly and gladly. And it is the same with food and friends and relatives and everything else that God may give or take away.

And that is why I think it better than everything that a man should abandon himself wholly to God, whatever it may be his will to impose on him, be it contempt or heavy labors or any other kind of suffering, so that he accepts it joyfully and thankfully, and lets himself be guided by God rather than trying to arrange things for himself. So if you will learn gladly from God and follow him, things will be all right for you. With such a disposition one can well accept honors and ease. But if hardships and disgrace come to a man, he must bear it and be glad to bear it. And so people can with every justification and right judgment eat well, if in the same spirit they would be prepared to fast.

And this is probably the reason God spares his friends many great sorrows; for his immeasurable faithfulness to them could not otherwise suffer it to be so, because so great and so many profits are contained in suffering, and he does not wish, nor would it be fitting, to let them lack such benefits. But he is content when their will is good and just. Were it not so, he would not permit them to escape any suffering because of the innumerable benefits suffering brings.

Therefore, so long as God is well content, be at peace; but if it pleases him that something different should happen with you, still be at peace. For inwardly a man ought to entrust himself so completely to God with his whole will that he is not greatly concerned about his way of life or the works he performs. And you ought especially to avoid anything extraordinary, whether in clothing or food or speech—such as indulging in fine talk—or extraordinary gestures, because this leads to nothing. But still you must know that not everything extraordinary is forbidden to you. There are many extraordinary things one has to do at certain times and among certain people, because if a man is extraordinary he must act in various extraordinary ways on many occasions.

A man ought to have formed his inward disposition in our Lord Jesus Christ in all respects, so that people can see in him a reflection of all our Lord's works and of his divine image; and within himself a man ought, so far as he can, to carry out a perfect imitation of all these works. You must work, and he ought to receive. Perform your works with all your devotion and all your intention; let this always be your disposition, and may you in all your works form yourself into him.

Counsel 19: Why God often permits good men, who are genuinely good, to be often hindered in their good works

Our faithful God often permits his friends to weaken so that any support on which they might depend or rely should be taken from them. For to a man who loves God it would be a great joy if he could perform many great deeds, perhaps keeping vigil or fasting or other exercises, and such remarkable, great, and difficult matters. To be able to do this is a great joy and a prop and gives hope, and it lends people support and help and confidence in their undertakings. But our Lord's will is to take this away from them, because he wants to be their only support and confidence. And his only reason for doing this is simply his goodness and mercy. God is not moved to perform any deed by anything other than his own goodness. Our deeds do not move him to give us anything or to do anything for us. Our Lord wants his friends to forget such false notions, and this is why he takes this support away from them: so that he may be their only support. For he wants to endow them richly, and this only out of his generous goodness; and he should be their support and comfort, and they should see and consider themselves as a mere nothing among all God's great gifts. For the more man's spirit, naked and empty, depends upon God and is preserved by him, the deeper is the man established in God, and the more receptive is he to God's finest gifts. For man should build upon God alone.

Counsel 20: Of the body of our Lord: how one should often receive it, and with what manner and devotion

Whoever would gladly receive the Body of our Lord ought not to wait until he discovers certain emotions or sensations in himself, or until his inwardness and devotion are great; but he ought to make sure that he has the proper will and intention. You should not attach such importance to what you feel; rather, consider important what you love and what you intend.

The man who freely wants and is able to go to our Lord should as the first condition have a conscience free from every reproach of sin. The second condition is that his will be turned to God, that he intends nothing and delights in nothing except in God and what is wholly godly, and that everything should displease him that is unlike God. And it is in this way, too, that a man should test how far away from God or how close to him he may be, and this will tell him how near or far away from God he is. The third condition is that his love for the blessed sacrament and for our Lord ought to grow in him more and more, and that his reverent awe for it should not decrease because of his frequent receiving; because often what is life for one man is death for another. Therefore you should observe whether your love for God grows and your reverence does not decrease; and then the oftener that you go to the sacrament, the better by far will you be, and the better and more profitable by far will it be for you. So do not let people talk and preach you away from your God; the oftener, the better, and the dearer to God. For it is our Lord's delight to dwell in man and with him.

Now you may say: "Alas, sir, I know how empty and cold and inert I am, and that is why I dare not go to our Lord!"

But what I say is, all the more reason for you to go to your God; for it is in him that you will be warmed and kindled, and in him you will be made holy, to him alone will you be joined and with him alone made one, for you will find that the sacrament possesses, as does nothing else, the grace by which your bodily strength will be united and collected through the wonderful power of our Lord's bodily presence, so that all man's distracted thoughts and intentions are here collected and united, and what was dispersed and debased is here raised up again and its due order restored as it is offered to God. The senses within are so informed by our indwelling God, and weened from the outward distractions of temporal things, and all at once become godly; and as your body is strengthened by his Body it becomes renewed. For we shall be changed into him and wholly united, so that what is his becomes ours, and all that is ours becomes his, our heart and his one heart, our body and his one Body. Our senses and our will, our intention, our powers and our members shall be so brought into him that we sense him and become aware of him in every power of our bodies and our souls.

Now you may say: "Alas, sir, I can find nothing better than poverty in myself. How could I dare go to him?"

Be sure of this, if you want all your poverty to be changed, then go to that abundant treasury of all immeasurable riches, and so you will be rich; for in your heart you should know that he alone is the treasure that can satisfy and fulfill you. So say: "This is why I want to come to you, that your riches may replenish my poverty, that your immeasurable wealth may fill out my emptiness, that your boundless and incomprehensible divinity may make good my so pitiful and decayed humanity."

"Alas, sir, I have committed so many sins that I cannot atone for them!"

Go to him for this, for he has made fitting atonement for all guilt. In him you may well offer up to the heavenly Father an offering worthy enough to atone for all your sins.

"Alas, sir, I should like to utter my praises, but I cannot!"

Go to him, for he only is the thanks the Father will accept and he alone is the immeasurable, truth-revealing, perfect praise of all the divine goodness.

In short, if you want all your sins to be wholly taken from you and to be clothed in virtues and graces, if you want to be led back joyfully to the source and to be guided by every virtue and grace, see to it that you are able to receive that sacrament worthily and often; so you will become one with him and be ennobled through his Body. Yes, in the Body of our Lord the soul is joined so close to God that not even the angels, not the cherubim or seraphim, can find or tell the difference between them. For as the angels approach God they approach the soul; as they approach the soul they approach God. There was never union so close; for the soul is far more closely united with God than are the body and soul that form one man. This union is far closer than if one were to pour a drop of water into a cask of wine; there, we still have water and wine, but here we have such a changing into one that there is no creature who can find the distinction.

Now, you may say: "How can this be? I don't feel anything of the kind."

What does that matter? The less that you feel and the more that you believe, the more praiseworthy is your faith, the more regarded, and the more praise will it receive, for a perfect faith is far more in a man than a mere supposing. In God we have true knowledge. In truth, all that we lack is true faith. We may think that what we feel benefits us more than faith, but that is only because we obey external rules. There is no more in the one than in the other. If a man believes constantly, he will receive constantly and possess constantly.

Now, you say: "How could I have faith in greater things when I am not disposed to this but know myself to be deficient and distracted by many things?"

Well, you ought to be aware of two properties in yourself that our Lord, too, had in him. He possessed superior and inferior powers, which in their turn performed two works; for his superior powers possessed and enjoyed everlasting blessedness, but at the same time here on earth his inferior powers were engaged in the greatest suffering and strife. Yet this working of the inferior powers did not deter the superior powers from attaining their object. It ought to be so in you: your superior powers should be elevated to God, wholly offered and bound to him. But beyond doubt we ought to consign all our sufferings to the body and the inferior powers and the senses; but the spirit ought with all its might to lift itself up, and then, liberated, sink down into its God. But the sufferings of the senses and of the inferior powers, and the opposition they meet, is not the spirit's concern; for the greater and the more violent the conflict is, the greater and more praiseworthy are the victory and its glory. For the greater the opposition, the more violent the onslaughts of vice, the more does man possess virtue if he conquers, and the dearer he is to God. And therefore, if you wish to receive your God worthily, be sure that your superior powers are directed toward your God and that your will is seeking his will, that you are intending him, and that your trust is based on him.

When a man is so disposed, he never receives the precious Body of our Lord without receiving extraordinary and great graces, and the oftener, the greater profit to him. Yes, a man might receive the Body of our Lord with such devotion and intention that if it were already ordained for him to come into the lowest order of angels, he might by so receiving on that one occasion be raised up into the next rank. Yes, you could receive him with such devotion that you might be seen in the eighth or in the ninth choir. And therefore, if there were two men alike in their whole lives, and one of them had received the Body of our Lord once more often than the other, through that he could appear like a shining sun in comparison with the other, and could receive a singular union with God.

This receiving and this blessed enjoyment of the Body of our Lord does not consist only in an external enjoyment. Its enjoyment is also spiritual, with a heart that yearns and in a union in devotion. A man may receive it in such faith that he becomes richer in graces than any other man on earth. A man may receive spiritually, whatever he may be, a thousand times and more in a day, whether he be sick or well. But one ought to approach such spiritual communion as the sacrament itself, according to the dictates of good order and with great longing. But even if one does not have the longing, one should incite it and prepare for it and act as it requires, and so one will become holy here in time and blessed there in eternity; for to go after God and to follow him, that is eternity. May the teacher of truth and the lover of chastity and the life of eternity grant us this. Amen.

Counsel 21: Of zeal

If a man wishes to receive the Body of our Lord, that should be done without any great anxiety. So it is fitting and very profitable to go to confession first, even if we have not incurred any blame, so that we may have the fruits of the sacrament of penance. But if it were the case that a man had incurred some blame, and it is difficult for him to go to confession, then let him have recourse to his God, and admit his guilt with great contrition, and then let him be at peace until he can make his confession. And if recollection of his sins or of their punishment intrude, then let him think that God, too, has forgotten them. It is God to whom we should confess sooner than to men, and if we are guilty of sin, it is our confession and our self-reproaches before God to which we should attend carefully. And if we want to go to the sacrament, we ought not to neglect this confession before God in favor of external penance, for it is what is in our intention as we perform our works that is just and godly and good.

People ought to learn to be free of their works as they perform them. For a man who has not practiced this, it is hard, learning to attain to a state in which the people around him and the works he performs are no hindrance—and much zeal is needed to achieve this—so that God is present to him and his light shines in him undiminished, whatever the occasion, whatever the environment. For this a lively zeal is needed, and, particularly, two things. One is that a man should have his inwardness well protected, and that his mind be on its guard against the images that surround him outside, keeping them out, never letting them intrude to occupy him and accompany him, never letting them find a home in him. The second is that a man should not allow himself to be weakened or distracted or alienated by any multiplicity—not by his own inward images, whether these be his own imaginings or an exaltation of his perceptions, nor by outward images or whatever else it may be that he has present to him. To this he ought to apply and turn all his power.

Now, you may say: "If a man is to perform outward works he must go outside himself, for no work can be accomplished except in the form that is proper to it."

That is indeed true. But to practiced men the outwardness of images is not outward because to inward men all things possess a divine inwardness.

Above all things, it is necessary that a man should apply and exercise his reason, firmly and constantly directing it toward God, and so always inwardly it will become divinized. To reason, nothing is as proper or as present or as close as God. Reason never turns itself in any other direction. It does not have recourse to creatures, unless it suffers violence and injustice, and it is then all broken down and distracted. If, in someone young—or whoever he may be—reason has suffered injury, great zeal must be used, and he must do all he can to coax reason back again and to tend and foster it. For however proper or natural God may be to reason, if people begin by misdirecting reason and making it rely upon creatures, perverting it into their forms and applying it to them, reason will lose some of its health and its power, and its noble intentions will be so hindered that all the zeal men can use is not too much for him to restore himself. When he has done all this, still he must be on constant guard.

Above everything else a man should see to it that he applies himself vigorously and well. If someone who does not apply and exercise himself wants to be and act like a man who applies himself, he will go completely astray, and nothing will become of him. Even if a man has begun by freeing and separating himself from all things, after that he can still perform all his works discerningly, learning to use them without possessiveness or to forgo them without distress. But if a man finds all his love and delight in something, and pursues it with all his will, whether it be food or drink or whatever else, this cannot but bring harm to an inexperienced man.

A man should accustom himself to seeking and wanting nothing for himself in anything, and to finding and accepting God in everything. For God does not give; he has never given any gift so that we might have it and then rest upon it, but all the gifts he ever gave in heaven and on earth he gave so that he might give us the one gift that is himself. With all these other gifts he wants to prepare us for the gift that he himself is. All the works God has ever performed in heaven and in earth he performed for the sake of one work, so that he might perform that, and it is to be himself blessed, so that he may make us blessed. Therefore I say: In every gift, in every work, we ought to learn to look toward God, and we should not allow ourselves to be satisfied or be detained by anything. Whatever our way of life may be, we must not cease to progress; this has been true for everyone, however far he might have advanced. Above all else, we should always be preparing ourselves, always renewing ourselves to receive God's gifts.

Let me tell you briefly about someone who greatly longed to obtain something from our Lord; but I said she was not nearly ready for it, and if God were to give her the gift, unready as she was, it would have been the ruin of her.

One may ask: "Why was she not ready? She had a good enough will; and do you not say that this can accomplish all things, and that in this everything and every perfection consist?"

That is true, but will is to be understood in two senses. There is one will that is accidental and inessential, another will that is determining, creative, habitual.

Indeed, it is not enough for a man's disposition to be detached just for the present moment when he wants to be bound to God, but he must have a well-exercised detachment from what is past and from what is yet to come. Then one is able to receive from God great things and, in the things, God. But if a man is not ready, the gift is ruined, and God with the gift. This is the reason God cannot always give us what we ask from him. This is no fault in him, for he is a thousand times swifter to give than we are to receive. But we do him violence and injustice, because we with our unreadiness are obstacles to the works that belong to his nature.

A man with all his gifts should learn to take himself out of himself, to keep nothing for himself, to seek nothing—not profit or delight or inward joy or sweetness or reward or the kingdom of heaven or his own will. God never gave himself or gives himself according to anyone else's will. He gives himself only by his own will. When God finds someone who is of one will with him, he gives himself to him and lets himself be in him, with everything that he is. And the more that we cease to belong to ourselves, the more truly do we belong to this. Therefore it is not enough for God that we should once surrender ourselves and all that we possess and can do, but we should renew this in ourselves again and again, uniting ourselves with him and emptying ourselves of self in all things.

And it is also very profitable for a man not to be content because he is disposed toward virtues such as obedience, poverty, and other such; rather, he should exercise the works and the fruits of these virtues, trying himself often, and he should wish and long for other people to exercise and try him. For it is not enough for a man to perform the works of virtue, or to practice obedience, or to accept poverty or contempt, or that he should in other ways humble or detach himself; rather, one must persist in this, never giving up, until one has gained the essence and the foundation of these virtues. And we can test whether we have them by this: when one finds oneself inclined above all else to virtue, and if one performs the works of virtue without preparing one's will, and if one carries them out without any special intention of obtaining some just or important matter, acting virtuously for virtue's own sake, for the love of virtue and no other reason—then one possesses the virtues perfectly, and not until then.

Let us go on learning to abandon ourselves until we hold on to nothing that is our own. All our tempests and strife come only from self-will, whether we see this or whether we do not. We should put ourselves and all that we are in a pure cessation of will and desire, into God's good and dearest will, with everything that we might will and desire in all things.

A question: "Ought one willingly to forgo even God's sweetness? Could that not come from inertia and from too little love for him?"

Yes, provided that one can recognize the distinction. If we want to know whether this comes from inertia, or from a true detachment, or from surrender to God's will, we ought to observe, when we experience such inward surrender, whether we find ourselves as faithful to God as ever we could be in times of great emotion, whether then we do all that we would at other times do, and not less, and whether we keep ourselves as detached from all consolations and helps as we would if we were to feel God himself present to us.

Then no time can be too short for a just man who is in perfect goodwill. For when the will is so disposed that it wants to accomplish every single thing of which it is capable—not just now, but if the man were to live for another thousand years, he would want to do all he was capable of—then the will gains as much as a thousand years of works could do; in God's eyes, he has all this.

Counsel 22: How man should follow God, and of a good manner of living

A man who wants to establish himself in a new life or a new way of working must go to his God, and with great force and with all devotion he must entreat of him that he will furnish him with what is best of all, with what is dearest and the greatest honor to God, and he must want and intend nothing for himself, but only God's dearest will and nothing else. Whatever God may then send him, let him accept it directly from God himself and let him regard it as the best of all that could come to him, and let him be wholly and utterly at peace in it.

And if later some other manner of living pleases him better, he ought to think: "God gave you this manner"; and so let it be the best that he could wish. In this he should have faith in God, and he should draw all that is good in other manners of living into this one manner, and accept everything, whatever its nature be, in this and according to this. For whatever good God has performed and endowed one manner with may also be found in all good manners; for one ought to take from one manner of living the good that is common to all of them and not what is peculiar to that one. For a man must always accomplish some one thing; he cannot do everything. It has to be one thing and in that one thing we ought to find everything. Because if a man wanted to do everything—this, that, and the other, leaving his own manner of living and taking on another that for the moment pleased him better—in truth that would produce great instability. For a man who has renounced the world and entered a religious order is more likely to achieve perfection than is someone who has left one order to join another, however holy he may have been. That is what changing one's way of life does. Let a man decide on one good way and persist in it, and introduce into it all ways that are good, and let him consider that he has received this way of life from God, and not set off today on one way and then tomorrow on another, and let him never be afraid that in doing this he is missing anything. Because with God one cannot miss anything; as little as God himself can, so little can man miss anything with God. Therefore accept some one thing from God, and into it bring everything that is good.

But if it happens that it cannot be that one thing can be reconciled with another, that is a certain sign for you that it is not from God. One good is not in opposition to another; for, as our Lord said: "Every kingdom which is divided in itself must perish" (Lk 11:17); and as he also said: "Who is not with me is against me, and he who does not gather with me scatters" (Mt 12:30). So let this be a certain sign for you: if something good cannot

tolerate another good thing—or, it may be, a less good thing—
then that is not from God. It ought to bring in and not disperse.

So it was said in a few true words that were added here: "Our
faithful God disposes the best of all for every man; of that there is
no doubt."

This is certainly true, and he never takes anyone lying down
whom he could have found standing upright, for God's goodness
intends all things for the very best.

Then I was asked why God did not therefore dispose for men
who, he knew, would fall from the grace of baptism to die in
childhood before they had reached years of discretion, since he
knew that they would fall and not rise again—would not that be
the very best for them?

So I said: God is no destroyer of any good thing, but rather he
brings it to perfection. God does not destroy nature; he perfects
it. And grace, too, does not destroy nature, but perfects it. If in
the beginning God had destroyed nature, it would have suffered
violence and injustice; and this God does not do. Man has a free
will, with which he may choose good and evil, and God offers
death in return for evil deeds, and in return for good deeds he
offers life. Man must be free, and the master of all his actions,
unimpeded and unconstrained. Grace does not destroy nature; it
perfects it. Glory does not destroy grace; it perfects it. For glory is
perfected grace. Therefore it is not in God to destroy anything that
has being, but rather he is a perfecter of all things. So we should
not destroy in ourselves any good thing, however small it may be,
even for the sake of something great, but we should rather bring
it to the greatest perfection.

Then we talked about one man who was supposed to be beginning a completely new life, and I said something like this: he ought to become a man who seeks for God and finds God in all things, always, everywhere, with everyone, in every way. Doing this, we can always go on growing and increasing, and never come to the end of our increasing.

Counsel 23: Of interior and exterior works

If a man wished to withdraw into himself with all his powers, interior and exterior, and if he could maintain this state in such a way that there was neither imagining nor activity in him, and he could remain free of all activities, interior or exterior, he ought to be on his guard in case this very state itself may become a form of activity. But if a man is not attracted toward works and does not want to be engaged in them, he ought to force himself to do something, whether it be an interior or exterior work, because he should not allow himself to become self-complacent in anything, however good it may seem or may be. If he experiences such struggle or compulsion that it seems that he is being acted upon rather than himself acting, so let him learn to cooperate with his God. He ought not to flee or deny or suspect his own inwardness. He should learn to work in it and with it and from it, so that he can transform inwardness into activity and bring his activities into his inwardness, and so that he can train himself to act in freedom. For we ought to keep our eye on this interior work and on what we produce from it: reading, praying, or, if need be, exterior activities. But if an exterior activity is hindering our interior work, we should prefer what is interior. But if both could exist together in one form of working, that would be the best—for man and God to work together.

Now, if it be asked: "How could a man cooperate in this way when he is detached from himself and from all works—as Saint Dionysius said, that man says the finest things about God who has learned out of the fullness of his inward riches to keep silence about him—and when for such a man images and works, praises and thanks, or anything else he could do have departed?"

The answer is that there is still one work that remains proper and his own, and that is annihilation of self. Yet this annihilation and diminution of the self, however great a work it may be, will remain uncompleted unless it is God who completes it in the self. Humility becomes perfected only when God humbles man with man's cooperation. When this happens, it is sufficient for the man and for the virtue, and not until then.

A question: "How should God annihilate a man, even with his cooperation? It would seem that man's annihilation would be his exaltation by God, for the Gospel says: 'Whoever humbles himself will be exalted'" (Mt 23:12).

Answer: yes, and no! A man ought to humble himself, and even that cannot be enough if God does not do it; and he ought to be exalted. Not that humbling is one thing and exaltation another; but rather the most exalted exaltedness of exaltation lies in the very depths of humility. The deeper and lower the depth is, the higher and more immeasurable the exaltation and the heights, and the deeper the fount, the higher it springs; height and depth are the same. Therefore, the more a man can humble himself, the higher he will be, and that is why our Lord said: "Whoever wants to be the greatest, let him become the least among you" (Mk 9:34). Whoever wants to be the one must become the other. Being this is learned only by becoming that. He who will become the least will in truth be the greatest, but he who has become the least is here and now the greatest of all. And so the words of the evangelist become true and fulfilled: "Whoever humbles himself will be exalted." For all our being consists in nothing but becoming nothing.

It is written: "You have become rich in all virtues" (1 Cor 1:5). Truly that can never happen until first one has become poor in all things. Whoever wants to receive everything must also renounce everything. That is a fair bargain and an equal return, as I said a while ago. Therefore, because God wants to give us himself and all things as our own free possessions, so he wants to deprive us, utterly and completely, of all possessiveness. Yes, truly, God in no way wants us to possess even as much as I could hold in my eye. For none of the gifts he ever gave us, neither gifts of nature nor gifts of grace, did he give for any other reason than that he wishes us to have nothing that is our own; and he never gave anything as their own to his mother or to any man or to any creature in any way at all. And so that he may teach us and make us aware of this, he often takes away from us both earthly and spiritual possessions, for it should not be for us but for him alone to possess them as honors. But we ought to have everything as if it were loaned to us and not given, without any possessiveness, whether it be our bodies or our souls, our minds, powers, worldly goods or honors, friends, kinsmen, houses, lands—all things.

What is God's intention in this which he considers so important?

Because he wants himself to be, solely and wholly, what we possess. This is what he wants, this is what he intends, this alone is important to him: that he may be and he must be this. In this consists his greatest delight and pleasure; and the more fully and generously he may be this, the greater are his delight and joy. For the more that we possess all things, the less do we possess him; and the less the love we have for all things, the more do we have him and all that he has to bestow. Therefore when our Lord wanted to speak about every form of blessedness, he put poverty of spirit at the head of them all; and it was put first as a sign that all blessedness and perfections together have their beginning in poverty of spirit. And truly, wherever that was the foundation, all good things could be built upon it, and without this there would be nothing.

If we strip ourselves of everything that is external, in return God wishes to give us as our own everything that is in heaven, and heaven itself with all its powers—yes, everything that has ever flowed out from him and that all the angels and saints possess—that it may be our own as much as it is theirs, and more our own than any external thing can be. In return for my going out of myself for love of him, God will wholly become my own, with all that he is and all that he can bestow, as much my own as his own, neither less nor more. He will be my own a thousandfold more than any man ever owned anything that he has in his coffer, more than he ever owned himself. Nothing was ever owned as much as God will be my own, with everything he can do and is.

We ought to earn the owning of this by living here without ownership of ourselves and of anything that is not God, and the more perfect and unimpeded this poverty is, so is our owning it more our own. We ought not to intend or look for such a return as this; we ought never to give one glance at whether we are going to gain or receive anything, but all should be for the love of virtue alone. The less we own, the more it is our own; as the great Paul says: "Possessing, we should be as if we possess nothing, and still we should possess all things" (2 Cor 6:10). A man is free of possessiveness who covets nothing, who wants to have nothing —not of himself, not of everything that is external to him, yes, not even of God or of all things.

Do you want to know what a truly poor man is like?

That man is truly poor in spirit who can well forgo everything that is not necessary. That is why the man who sat naked in the barrel said to the great Alexander, who had all the world subject to him: "I am a far greater lord than you, for I have despised more than you have possessed. All the things that you thought so great that you wanted them were too little for me to despise." He is more blessed who can forgo all things and has no need of them than is the man who possessed everything and needed it. The best man is the one who can forgo what he does not need. Therefore the man who can best of all forgo and despise has forsaken most of all. We think it something great that a man should for the love of God give a thousand gold marks and with his riches build convents and monasteries and feed all the poor; that would be something great. But a man would be far more blessed who for the love of God despised all this. A man would possess a truly heavenly kingdom who knew how to renounce everything for God, whatever God might or might not give him.

Then you say: "Yes, sir, but would not I, with my shortcomings, be an occasion of possessiveness or a hindrance to true poverty?"

If you have shortcomings, ask God earnestly to take them away, if that be to his glory and pleasing to him, because without him you can do nothing. If he takes them away, then thank him; and if he does not do this, suffer it for his love, but not as a shortcoming through sin, but rather as a good exercise through which you will gain reward and exercise patience. You must be at peace, whether he gives you his gifts or not.

God gives to every man according to what is best and most fitting for him. If you are making a coat for someone, you must make it to his measure; what fits one man will not fit another at all. You take everyone's measure, and then it fits him. And so God gives to everyone the very best that he sees to be closest to his needs. Truly, anyone who trusts God completely in this accepts and receives as much from his smallest gift as from the greatest of all. If God wanted to give me what he gave Saint Paul, I should be glad to accept it, if that were his will. But since he does not want to give me that—for there are very few people whom he wishes to know so much in this life—he is as dear to me, I pay him as much thanks and I am as much at peace because God does not give it to me, that he withholds it from me, as if he were giving it to me. I am as satisfied and well pleased with that as if he were to give it to me, if either be acceptable to me. Truly, this is how God's will ought to content me: everything God might wish to do or to give ought to be to me so dear and so precious, because it is so according to his will, that for him not to give me the gift, not to do the thing, would be as pleasing to me as if he did. So all God's gifts and all his deeds would be mine, and let every created thing do its best, or its worst, they could deprive me of nothing of this. So what do I have to complain about if all men's gifts are mine? In truth, I am so well contented with what God does or does not give to me and do for me that I would not pay a copper penny for being able to live the finest life I could think of.

Now, you say: "I am afraid that I am not working as hard as I ought at this and I am not keeping it up as I could."

Accept it as suffering, suffer it patiently, take it as an exercise, and be at peace. God is glad to suffer shame and adversity and is happy to forgo service and praise so that they who intend and obey him should possess him in peace. Why should we not be at peace, whatever he may give us or whatever we may lack? It is written and our Lord says: "They are blessed who suffer for the sake of justice" (Mt 5:10). Truly, if there were a thief whom they were about to hang who deserved to hang because he had stolen, and if there were another who had committed murder and whom justly they were going to break on the wheel—if these two found it in themselves to say: "Look, what you will suffer is for the sake of justice, for they are treating you justly," they would at once be blessed.

In truth, however unjust we may be, if we accept from God whatever he may or may not do to us as justice, and suffer it for justice's sake, then we shall be blessed. So do not complain about anything; all you need to complain about is that you go on complaining and that nothing satisfies you. All that you should complain about is that you have too much. Anyone properly disposed would accept want as if it were plenty.

Now, you say: "Alas, God does such great things in lots of people, and they become so transmuted in the divine life, and God does all this in them and they do nothing."

Thank God for what he does in them, and if he gives this to you, take it, for God's sake; and if he does not give it, then you ought willingly to lack it, and intend nothing but him, and do not be upset, whether God does your works for you or whether you perform them yourself; because if you intend God alone, he must perform them whether he like it or not.

Do not upset yourself, whatever form of life or devotion God may give to anyone. If I were so good and holy that they had to raise me to the altars with the saints, still people would be talking and worrying about whether this was grace or nature working in me, and puzzling themselves about it. They are all wrong in this. Leave God to work in you; let him do it, and do not be upset over whether he is working with nature or above nature, for nature and grace are both his. What has that to do with you—what it suits him to work with, or what he may work in you or in someone else? He must work how or where or in what way it is fitting to him.

There was a man who would dearly have liked to make a stream flow through his garden, and he said: "If the water could be mine, I should not care what sort of channel brought it to me, iron or timber, bone or rusty metal, if only I could have the water." And so anyone is quite wrong who worries about the means through which God is working his works in him, whether it be nature or grace. Just let God work, and just be at peace.

For as much as you are in God, so much are you at peace, and as far as you are distant from God, so far are you from peace. Whatever is in God, it has peace. As much in God, so much in peace. So see by this how much you are in God, or if you are not, whether you are or are not at peace; for if you are not at peace, there cannot then be peace in you, for lack of peace comes from created things and not from God. And there is nothing in God that is to be feared; everything that is in God is only to be loved. And so there is nothing in him that is to be mourned.

He who has all his will and his wish has all his joy; and no one has this whose will is not wholly one with the will of God. May God grant us this union. Amen.

SELECTED SERMONS

Sermon 6

"The just will live forever, and their reward is with God" (Ws 5:16). See exactly what this means; though it may sound simple and commonplace, it is really noteworthy and excellent.

"The just will live." Which are the just? Somewhere it is written: "That man is just who gives everyone what belongs to him"—those who give God what is his, and the saints and the angels what is theirs, and their fellow man what is his.

 Honor belongs to God. Who are those who honor God? Those who have wholly gone out of themselves, and who do not seek for what is theirs in anything, whatever it may be, great or little; who are not looking beneath themselves or above themselves or beside themselves or at themselves; who are not desiring possessions or honors or ease or pleasure or profit or inwardness or holiness or reward or the kingdom of heaven; and who have gone out from all this, from everything that is theirs—these people pay honor to God, and they honor God properly, and they give him what is his.

People ought to give joy to the angels and the saints. What, does this amaze you? Can a man in this life give joy to those who are in everlasting life? Yes, indeed he can! Every saint has such great delight and such unspeakable joy from every good work; from a good will or an aspiration they have such great joy that no tongue can tell, no heart can think how great is the joy they have from this. Why is that? Because their love for God is so immeasurably great, and they have so true a love for him, that his honor is dearer to them than their blessedness. And not only the saints or the angels, for God himself takes such delight in this, just as if it were his blessedness; and his being depends upon it, and his contentment and his well-being. Yes, mark this well: if we do not want to serve God for any other reason than the great joy they have in this who are in everlasting life, and that God himself has, we could do it gladly and with all our might.

And one ought also to give help and support to those who are in purgatory, and also improvement and edification to those who are still living.

Such a man is just in one way, and so in another sense are all those who accept all things alike from God, whatever it may be, great or small, joy or sorrow, all of it alike, less or more, one like the other. If you account anything more than something else, you do wrong. You ought to go wholly out from your own will.

Recently I had this thought: if God did not wish as I do, then I would still wish as he does. There are some people who want to have their own will in everything; that is bad, and there is much harm in it. Those are a little better who do want what God wants, and want nothing contrary to his will; if they were sick, what they would wish would be for God's will to be for them to be well. So these people want God to want according to their will, not for themselves to want according to his will. One has to endure this, but still it is wrong. The just have no will at all; what God wills is all the same to them, however great distress that may be.

For just men, the pursuit of justice is so imperative that if God were not just, they would not give a fig for God; and they stand

fast by justice, and they have gone out of themselves so completely that they have no regard for the pains of hell or the joys of
heaven or for any other thing. Yes, if all the pains that those have
who are in hell, men or devils, or all the pains that have ever been
or ever will be suffered on earth were to be joined on to justice,
they would not give a straw for that, so fast do they stand by God
and by justice. Nothing is more painful or hard for a just man
than what is contrary to justice. In what way? If one thing gives
them joy and another sorrow, they are not just; but if on one
occasion they are joyful, then they are always joyful; and if on
one occasion they are more joyful and on others less, then they
are wrong. Whoever loves justice stands so fast by it that whatever
he loves, that is his being; nothing can deflect him from this, nor
does he esteem anything differently. Saint Augustine says: "When
the soul loves, it is more properly itself than when it gives life."
This sounds simple and commonplace, and yet few understand
what it means; and still it is true. Anyone who has discernment in
justice and in just men—he understands everything I am saying.

"The just will live." Among all things there is nothing so dear
or so desirable as life. However wretched or hard his life may be,
a man still wants to live. It is written somewhere that the closer
anything is to death, the more it suffers. Yet however wretched life
may be, still it wants to live. Why do you eat? Why do you sleep?
So that you live. Why do you want riches or honors? That you
know very well; but—why do you live? So as to live. And still you
do not know why you live. Life is in itself so desirable that we
desire it for its own sake. Those in hell are in everlasting torment,

but they would not want to lose their lives, not the devils or the souls of men, for their life is so precious that it flows without any medium from God into the soul. And because it flows from God without medium, they want to live. What is life? God's being is my life. If my life is God's being, then God's existence must be my existence and God's is-ness is my is-ness, neither less nor more.

They live eternally "with God," directly close to God, not beneath or above. They perform all their works with God, and God with them. As Saint John says: "The Word was with God" (Jn 1:1). It was wholly equal, and it was close beside—not beneath there or above there, but just equal. When God made man, he made woman from man's side, so that she might be equal to him. He did not make her out of man's head or his feet, so that she would be neither woman nor man for him, but so that she might be equal. So should the just soul be equal with God and close beside God, equal beside him, not beneath or above.

Who are they who are thus equal? Those who are equal to nothing, they alone are equal to God. The divine being is equal to nothing, and in it there is neither image nor form. To the souls who are equal, the Father gives equally, and he withholds nothing at all from them. Whatever the Father can achieve, that he gives equally to this soul—yes, if it no longer equals itself more than anything else, and it should not be closer to itself than to anything else. It should desire or heed its own honor, its profit, and whatever may be its own no more than what is a stranger's. Whatever belongs to anyone should not be distant or strange to the soul, whether this be evil or good. All the love of this world is founded on self-love. If you had forsaken that, you would have forsaken the whole world.

The Father gives birth to his Son in eternity, equal to himself. "The Word was with God, and God was the Word" (Jn 1:1); it was the same in the same nature. Yet I say more: he has given birth to him in my soul. Not only is the soul with him, and he equal with it, but he is in it, and the Father gives his Son birth in the soul in the same way that he gives him birth in eternity, and not otherwise. He must do it whether he likes it or not. The Father gives birth to his Son without ceasing; and I say more: he gives me birth—me, his Son and the same Son. I say more: He gives birth not only to me, his Son, but he gives birth to me as himself and himself as me and to me as his being and nature. In the innermost source, there I spring out in the Holy Spirit, where there is one life and one being and one work. Everything God performs is one; therefore he gives me, his Son, birth without any distinction. My fleshly father is not actually my father except in one little portion of his nature, and I am separated from him; he may be dead and I alive. Therefore the heavenly Father is truly my Father, for I am his Son and have everything that I have from him, and I am the same Son and not a different one. Because the Father performs one work, therefore his work is me, his Only Begotten Son, without any difference.

"We shall be completely transformed and changed into God" (2 Cor 3:18). See a comparison. In the same way, when in the sacrament bread is changed into the Body of our Lord, however many pieces of bread there were, they still become one Body. Just so, if all the pieces of bread were changed into my finger, there would still not be more than one finger. But if my finger were changed into the bread, there would be as many of one as of the other. What is changed into something else becomes one with it. I am so changed into him that he produces his being in me as one, not just similar. By the living God, this is true! There is no distinction.

The Father gives his Son birth without ceasing. Once the Son has been born he receives nothing from the Father because he has it all, but what he receives from the Father is his being born. In this we ought not to ask for something from God as if he were a stranger. Our Lord said to his disciples: "I have not called you servants, but friends" (Jn 15:14). Whoever asks for something from someone else is a servant, and he who grants it is a master. Recently I considered whether there was anything I would take or ask from God. I shall take careful thought about this, because if I were accepting anything from God, I should be subject to him as a servant, and he in giving would be as a master. We shall not be so in life everlasting.

Once I said here, and what I said is true: if a man obtains or accepts something from outside himself, he is in this wrong. One should not accept or esteem God as being outside oneself, but as one's own and as what is within one; nor should one serve or labor for any recompense, not for God or for his honor or for anything that is outside oneself, but only for that which one's own being and one's own life is within one. Some simple people think that they will see God as if he were standing there and they here. It is not so. God and I, we are one. I accept God into me in knowing; I go into God in loving. There are some who say that blessedness consists not in knowing but in willing. They are wrong; for if it consisted only in the will, it would not be one. Working and becoming are one. If a carpenter does not work, nothing becomes of the house. If the ax is not doing anything, nothing is becoming anything. In this working, God and I are one; he is working and I am becoming. The fire changes anything into itself that is put into it, and this takes on fire's own nature. The wood does not change the fire into itself, but the fire changes the wood into itself. So are we changed into God, that we shall know him as he is (1 Jn 3:2). Saint Paul says: "So shall we come to know him, I knowing him just as he knows me" (1 Cor 13:12), neither less nor more, perfectly equal. "The just will live forever, and their reward is with God," perfectly equal.

That we may love justice, for its own sake and for God, without asking return, may God help us to this. Amen.

Sermon 15

These words are written in the Gospel, and in German they mean: "There was a noble man who went into a foreign land, away from himself, and he came back home richer" (Lk 19:12). Now, in one Gospel we read that Christ said: "No one can be my disciple unless he follow me" (Lk 14:27) and forsake himself and keep nothing for himself, and then he will have everything, for to have nothing is to have everything. But to submit oneself to God with one's desire and one's heart, to make one's will wholly God's will, never once to look upon created things— anyone who had so forsaken himself, he would truly be given back to himself.

Goodness in itself, only goodness, does not bring peace to the soul. . . . If God were to give me anything without his will, I should not esteem it; but the very least that God gives me by his will—that gives me blessedness.

All created things have flowed out of God's will. If I were able only to long for God's goodness, his will is so noble that the Holy Spirit is flowing from his will without a medium. All good flows out from the overflowing of the goodness of God. Yes, God's will has savor for me only in his unity, where God's peace is for the goodness of all created things. In this unity, goodness and everything that ever gained being and life have peace, as in their last end. There you must love the Holy Spirit, as he is there, in unity—not in himself, but there where he, alone with God's goodness, has savor in that unity from which all goodness flows out of the overflowing of the goodness of God. Such a man "comes back home richer" than he went out. Whoever had so gone out of himself would be given back again to himself, more his own, and all the things he had in multiplicity and forsook will be wholly given back again to him in unity, for he will find himself and all things in the present now of unity. And anyone who had so gone out would come back home far more noble than he went out. This man lives now in utter freedom and a pure nakedness, for there is nothing that he must make subject to himself or that he must acquire, be it little or much, for everything that is God's own is his own.

The sun in its highest part corresponds to God in his unfathomable depths, in his depths of humility. Yes, the humble man does not need to entreat, but he can indeed command, for the heights of the divinity cannot look down except into the depths of humility, for the humble man and God are one and not two. This humble man has as much power over God as he has over himself; and all the good that is in all the angels and in all the saints is all his own, as it is God's own. God and this humble man are wholly one, and not two; for what God performs, he performs, too; and what God wishes, he wishes, too; and what God is, he is, too—one life and one being. Yes, by God! If this man were in hell, God would have to come down to him in hell, and hell would have to be for him the kingdom of heaven. God must of necessity do this; he would be compelled so that he had to do it, for then this man is divine being, and divine being is this man. For here, from the unity of God and from the humble man, there comes the kiss; for the virtue that is called humility is a root in the ground of the divinity in which it was planted, so that the virtue has its being only in the eternal One and nowhere else. I said in Paris in the schools that all things would be perfected in the truly humble man; and therefore I say that for the truly humble man nothing can be harmful, nothing can lead him astray. For there is nothing that does not flee what can annihilate it. All created things flee this, for they are nothing at all in themselves; and therefore the humble man flees everything that could lead him astray from God. This is why I flee from burning coals: because they want to destroy me, because they want to rob me of my being.

Scripture said: "A man went out." Aristotle began to write a book in which he wanted to discuss all things. Now, observe what Aristotle said about this man. Homo means as much as a "man" who has been endowed with form, and this gives him being and life with all created things, rational and irrational—irrational with all corporeal creatures and rational with the angels. And he says: "Just as all created things, with their images and forms, are comprehended in the rational angels, and the angels know with reason every differentiated thing—which gives the angel such delight that it would be amazing for those who had not experienced and tasted this—so man understands rationally the image and form of all created differentiated things." Aristotle said that the attribute of a man that makes him to be a man is that he understands all images and forms; because of this a man is a man, and that was the highest characteristic with which Aristotle could characterize a man.

Now, I, too, want to demonstrate what a man is. Homo means as much as a "man" to whom substance has been given, which gives him being and life and a rational being. A rational man is one who comprehends himself rationally, and who is himself separated from all matter and forms. The more he is separated from all things and turned into himself, the more he knows all things clearly and rationally within himself, without going outside; and the more he is a man.

Now, I ask: how can it be that separation of the understanding from form and image understands all things in itself, without going out from or changing itself? I reply: this comes from its simplicity, for the more purely simple a man's self is in itself, the more simply does he in himself understand all multiplicity, and he remains unchangeable in himself. Boethius says that God is an immovable good, standing still in himself, untouched and unmoved and moving all things. A simple understanding is in itself so pure that it understands the pure, naked divine being without a medium. And in the inflowing it receives divine nature just as do the angels, and in this the angels receive great joy. For anyone to be able to see an angel, he should be willing to be a thousand years in hell; but this understanding is in itself so pure and so clear that whatever one might see in this light would be an angel.

Now, notice carefully what Aristotle says about separated spirits in the book called *Metaphysics*. He is the greatest of the authorities who ever spoke about the natural sciences, and he deals with these separated spirits and says that they are not the form of anything, and that they accept their being as it flows without medium from God; and so they flow back in again, and receive the outflowing from God without medium, above the angels, and they contemplate God's naked being without distinction. This pure naked being Aristotle calls a "something." This is the most sublime thing that Aristotle ever said about the natural sciences, and no authority can say anything more sublime than this, unless he were to speak in the Holy Spirit. Now, I say that for this noble man the substance that the angels understood without form and on which they depend without medium is not sufficient; nothing but the Simple One suffices him.

I have also said more about the first beginning and the last end. The Father is a beginning of the divinity, for he understands himself in himself, and out of this the Eternal Word proceeds and yet remains within, and the Holy Spirit flows from them both, remaining within and unbegetting; for insofar as he remains within, he is an end of the divinity and of all created things; he is a pure repose and a resting of all that being ever acquired. The beginning is for the sake of the end, for in the last end is the repose of everything that rational being ever acquired. The last end of being is the darkness or the unknownness of the hidden divinity, in which this light shines that the darkness does not comprehend. Therefore Moses said: "He who is sent me" (Ex 3:14), he who is without name, who is a denial of all names and who never acquired a name. And therefore the prophet said: "Truly you are the hidden God" (Is 45:15), in the ground of the soul, where God's ground and the soul's ground are one ground. The more one seeks you, the less one finds you. You should so seek him that you find him nowhere. If you do not seek him, then you will find him. That we may so seek him that we may eternally remain with him—may God help us to this. Amen.

Sermon 22

The Latin text that I have read is written in the holy Gospel, and its meaning in German is: "Greetings to you, full of grace; the Lord is with you" (Lk 1:28). The Holy Spirit will come down from above the highest throne, and will enter into you from the light of the eternal Father.

There are three things here to understand: first, the lowliness of the angelic nature; second, that he acknowledged himself unworthy to name the mother of God; third, that he did not speak the word only to her, but that he spoke it to a great multitude, to every good soul that longs for God.

I say this: if Mary had not first given spiritual birth to God, he would never have been born bodily from her. A woman said to our Lord: "Blessed is the womb that bore you" (Lk 11:27). Then our Lord said: "It is not only the womb which bore me that is blessed; they are blessed who hear God's word and keep it" (Lk 11:28). It is more precious to God to be born spiritually from every such virgin or from every good soul than that he was bodily born of Mary.

In this we must understand that we must be an only son whom the Father has eternally begotten. When the Father begot all created things, then he begot me, and I flowed out with all created things, and yet I remained within, in the Father. In the same way, when the word that I am now speaking springs up in me, there is a second process as I rest upon the image, and a third when I pronounce it and you all receive it; and yet properly it remains within me. So I have remained within the Father. In the Father are the images of all created things. This piece of wood has a rational image in God. It is not merely rational, but it is pure reason.

The greatest good that God ever performed for man was that he became man. I ought to tell a story now that is very apposite here. There were a rich husband and wife. Then the wife suffered a misfortune through which she lost an eye, and she was much distressed by this. Then her husband came to her and said: "Madam, why are you so distressed? You should not distress yourself so, because you have lost your eye." Then she said: "Sir, I am not distressing myself about the fact that I have lost my eye; what distresses me is that it seems to me that you will love me less because of it." Then he said: "Madam, I do love you." Not long after that he gouged out one of his own eyes and came to his wife and said: "Madam, to make you believe that I love you, I have made myself like you; now I, too, have only one eye." This stands for man, who could scarcely believe that God loved him so much, until God gouged out one of his own eyes and took upon himself human nature. This is what "being made flesh" (Jn 1:14) is. Our Lady said: "How should this happen?" Then the angel said: "The Holy Spirit will come down from above into you" (Lk 1:34–35), from the highest throne, from the Father of eternal light.

"A child is born to us, a son is given to us" (Is 9:6), a child in the smallness of its human nature, a Son in its everlasting divinity. The authorities say: "All created things behave as they do because they want to give birth and they want to resemble the Father." Another authority says: "Every being that acts, acts for the sake of its end, that in its end it may find rest and repose." One authority says: "All created things act according to their first purity and according to their highest perfection." Fire as fire does not burn; it is so pure and so fine that it does not burn; but it is fire's nature that burns and pours its nature and its brightness according to its highest perfection into the dry wood. God has acted like this. He created the soul according to the highest perfection, and poured into it in its first purity all his brightness, and yet he has remained unmixed.

Recently I said in another place: "When God created all things, even if God had not before begotten anything that was uncreated, that carried within itself the images of all created things; that is the spark"—as I said before in the Maccabees' church (as you heard, if you were listening)—"and this little spark is so closely akin to God that it is an undivided simple one, and bears within itself the images of all created things, images without images and images beyond images."

Yesterday in the school among the important clerics there was a disputation. "I am surprised," I said: "that scripture is so rich that no one can fathom the least word in it." Now, if you ask me, since I am an only son whom the heavenly Father has eternally born, if then I have eternally been a son in God, then I say: "Yes and no. Yes, a son, as the Father has eternally borne me, and not a son, as to being unborn."

"In the beginning" (Jn 1:1). Here we are given to understand that we are an only son whom the Father has eternally borne out of the concealed darkness of the eternal concealment, remaining within in the first beginning of the first purity, which is a plenitude of all purity. Here I had my everlasting rest and sleep, in the eternal Father's hidden knowledge, remaining unspoken within. Out of the purity he everlastingly bore me, his only born son into that same image of his eternal Fatherhood, that I may be Father and give birth to him of whom I am born. It is just as if someone were to stand before a high cliff and were to shout: "Are you there?" The echo of his voice would shout back: "Are you there?" If he were to say: "Come out of there!" the echo, too, would say: "Come out of there!" Yes, if someone saw a piece of wood in that light, it would become an angel and a rational being; and not merely rational: it would become pure reason in primal purity, for there is the plenitude of all purity. God acts like that: he gives birth to his Only Begotten Son in the highest part of the soul. And as he gives birth to his Only Begotten Son into me, so I give him birth again into the Father. That was not different from when God gave birth to the angel while he was born of the Virgin.

I wondered—this is many years ago—whether I would be asked how it is that each blade of grass can be so different from the others; and it did happen that I was asked how they could be so different. I said: "What is more surprising is how they are all so alike." An authority said that the fact that all blades of grass are so different comes from the superabundance of God's goodness, which he pours superabundantly into all created things, so that his supremacy may be the more revealed. When I said: "It is more surprising that all the blades of grass are so alike," I went on: "Just as all angels in the primal purity are all one angel, so are all blades of grass one in the primal purity, and all things there are one."

As I was coming here, I was thinking that in temporal existence man can reach the point where he is able to compel God. If
I were up here, and I said to someone: "Come up here," that
would be difficult. But if I were to say: "Sit down there," that
would be easy. God acts like that. If a man humbles himself, God
cannot withhold his own goodness but must come down and
flow into the humble man, and to him who is least of all he gives
himself the most of all, and he gives himself to him completely.
What God gives is his being, and his being is his goodness, and
his goodness is his love. All sorrow and all joy come from love.
On the way, when I had to come here, I was thinking that I did
not want to come here because I would become wet with tears of
love. If you have ever been all wet with tears of love, let us leave
that aside for now. Joy and sorrow come from love. A man ought
not to fear God, for whoever fears him flees from him. This fear is
a harmful fear. There is a rightful fear, when someone fears that
he may lose God. A man should not fear him; he should love him,
for God loves man with all his supreme perfection. The authorities say that all things work with the intention of giving birth and
want to resemble the Father. They say: "The earth flees the heavens. If it flees downward, it comes down to the heavens; if it flees
upward, it comes to the lowest part of the heavens." The earth can
flee nowhere so deep that the heavens will not flow into it and
impress their powers on it and make it fruitful, whether it likes
this or not. This is how a man acts when he thinks that he can flee
from God, and yet he cannot flee from him; every corner where
he may go reveals God to him. He thinks that he is fleeing God,

and he runs into his lap. God bears his Only Begotten Son in you, whether you like it or not. Whether you are sleeping or waking, he does his part. Recently I asked whose fault it is if a man does not taste this, and I said that the fault was that his tongue was coated with some impurity—that is, with created things—just as with a man to whom all food is bitter and for whom nothing tastes good. Whose fault is it that food does not taste good to us? The fault is that we have no salt. The salt is divine love. If we had divine love, God would taste good to us, and all the works God ever performed, and we should receive all things from God, and we should perform all the same works that he performs. In this likeness we are all one single Son.

When God created the soul, he created it according to his highest perfection, so that it might be a bride of the Only Begotten Son. Because he knew this, he wanted to come forth from the secret treasure chamber of the eternal Fatherhood, in which he had eternally slept, unspoken, remaining within. "In the beginning." In the first beginning of the primal purity the Son had set up the pavilion of his everlasting glory, and he came out from there, from what was most exalted of all, because he wanted to exalt his beloved, whom the Father had eternally betrothed with him, so that he might bring her back again into the exaltation from which she came. Elsewhere it is written: "See! Your king is coming to you" (Zec 9:9). This is why he came out, and came leaping like a young hart (Sg 2:9), and suffered his torments for love, and he did not go out without wishing to go in again, into his chamber with his bride. This chamber is the silent darkness of the hidden Fatherhood. When he went out from the highest place of all, he wanted to go in again with his bride to the purest place of all, and wanted to reveal to her the hidden secret of his hidden divinity, where he takes his rest with himself and with all created things.

In *principio* means in German as much as a beginning of all being, as I said in the school. I said more: it is an end of all being, for the first beginning is for the sake of the last end. Yes, God never takes rest there where he is the first beginning; he takes rest there where he is an end and a repose of all being—not that this being should perish, but rather it is there perfected in its last end according to its highest perfection. What is the last end? It is the hidden darkness of the eternal divinity, and it is unknown, and it was never known, and it will never be known. God remains there within himself, unknown, and the light of the eternal Father has eternally shone in there, and the darkness does not comprehend the light (Jn 1:5). May the truth of which I have spoken help us, that we may come to this truth. Amen.

Sermon 48

An authority says: "All things that are alike love one another and unite with one another, and all things that are unlike flee from one another and hate one another." And one authority says that nothing is so unlike as are heaven and earth. The kingdom of earth was endowed by nature with being far off from heaven and unlike it. This is why earth fled to the lowest place and is immovable: so that it may not approach heaven. Heaven by nature apprehended that the earth fled from it and occupied the lowest place. Therefore heaven always pours itself out fruitfully upon the kingdom of earth; and the authorities maintain that the broad and wide heaven does not retain for itself so much as the width of a needle's point, but rather bestows it upon the earth. That is why earth is called the most fruitful of all created things that exist in time.

I say the same about the man who has annihilated himself in himself and in God and in all created things: this man has taken possession of the lowest place, and God must pour the whole of himself into this man, or else he is not God. I say in the truth, which is good and eternal and enduring, that God must pour out the whole of himself with all his might so totally into every man who has utterly abandoned himself that God withholds nothing of his being or his nature or his entire divinity, but he must pour all of it fruitfully into the man who has abandoned himself for God and has occupied the lowest place.

As I was coming here today I was wondering how I should preach to you so that it would make sense and you would understand it. Then I thought of a comparison; if you could understand that, you would understand my meaning and the basis of all my thinking in everything I have ever preached. The comparison concerns my eyes and a piece of wood. If my eye is open, it is an eye; if it is closed, it is the same eye. It is not the wood that comes and goes, but it is my vision of it. Now, pay good heed to me! If it happens that my eye is in itself one and simple (Mt 6:22), and it is opened and casts its glance upon the piece of wood, the eye and the wood remain what they are, and yet in the act of vision they become as one, so that we can truly say that my eye is the wood and the wood is my eye. But if the wood were immaterial, purely spiritual as is the sight of my eye, then one could truly say that in the act of vision the wood and my eye subsisted in one being. If this is true of physical objects, it is far truer of spiritual objects. You should know that my eye has far more in common with the eye of a sheep that is on the other side of the sea and that I never saw than it has in common with my ears, with which, however, it shares its being; and that is because the action of the sheep's eye is also that of my eye. And so I attribute to both more in common in their action than I do to my eyes and my ears, because their actions are different.

Sometimes I have spoken of a light that is uncreated and not capable of creation and that is in the soul. I always mention this light in my sermons. And this same light comprehends God without a medium—uncovered, naked, as he is in himself; and this comprehension is to be understood as happening when the birth takes place. Here I may truly say that this light may have more unity with God than it has with any power of the soul, with which, however, it is one in being. For you should know that this light is not nobler in my soul's being than is the feeblest or crudest power, such as hearing or sight or anything else that can be affected by hunger or thirst, frost or heat; and the simplicity of my being is the cause of that. Because of this, if we take the powers as they are in our being, they are all equally noble; but if we take them as they work, one is much nobler and higher than another.

That is why I say that if a man will turn away from himself and from all created things, by so much will he be made one and blessed in the spark in the soul, which has never touched either time or place. This spark rejects all created things, and wants nothing but its naked God, as he is in himself. It is not content with the Father or the Son or the Holy Spirit, or with the three Persons as far as each of them persists in his properties. I say truly that this light is not content with the divine nature's generative or fruitful qualities. I will say more, surprising though this is. I say in all truth, truth that is eternal and enduring, that this same light is not content with the simple divine essence in its repose, as it neither gives nor receives; but it wants to know the source of this essence; it wants to go into the simple ground, into the quiet desert, into which distinction never gazed—not the Father, nor the Son, nor the Holy Spirit. In the innermost part, where no one dwells, there is contentment for that light, and there it is more inward than it can be to itself, for this ground is a simple silence, in itself immovable, and by this immovability all things are moved, all life is received by those who in themselves have rational being.

May that enduring truth of which I have spoken help us that we may so have rational life. Amen.

Sermon 52

Blessedness opened its mouth to wisdom and said: "Blessed are the poor in spirit, for the kingdom of heaven is theirs" (Mt 5:3).

All angels and all saints and all who were ever born must keep silent when the Wisdom of the Father speaks, for all the Wisdom of the angels and of all created beings is mere folly before the unfathomable Wisdom of God. It has said that the poor are blessed.

Now, there are two kinds of poverty. There is an external poverty, which is good and is greatly to be esteemed in a man who voluntarily practices it for the love of our Lord Jesus Christ, for he himself used it when he was on earth. I do not now want to say anything more about this poverty. But there is a different poverty, an inward poverty, and it is of this that we must understand that our Lord is speaking: "Blessed are the poor in spirit."

Now, I beg you to be disposed to what I say; for I say to you in everlasting truth that if you are unlike this truth of which we want to speak, you cannot understand me. Various people have asked me what poverty may be in itself and what a poor man may be. Let us try to answer this.

Bishop Albert says that a poor man is one who does not find satisfaction in all the things God created; and this is well said. But we can put it even better, and take poverty in a higher sense. A poor man wants nothing, and knows nothing, and has nothing. Let us now talk about these three points; and I beg you for the sake of God's love that you understand this truth if you can, and if you do not understand it, do not burden yourself with it, for the truth I want to expound is such that there will be few good people to understand it.

First let us discuss a poor man as one who wants nothing. There are some people who do not understand this well. They are those who are attached to their own penances and external exercises, which seem important to people. God help those who hold divine truth in such low esteem! Such people present an outward picture that gives them the name of saints; but inside they are donkeys, for they cannot distinguish divine truth. These people say that a man is poor who wants nothing; but they interpret it in this way: that a man ought to live so that he never fulfills his own will in anything, but that he ought to comport himself so that he may fulfill God's dearest will. Such people are in the right, for their intention is good. For this let us commend them. May God in his mercy grant them the kingdom of heaven. But I speak in the divine truth when I say that they are not poor men, nor do they resemble poor men. They have great esteem in the sight of men who know no better, but I say that they are donkeys who have no understanding of divine truth. They deserve the kingdom of heaven for their good intention, but of the poverty of which we want to talk they know nothing.

If someone asks me now what kind of poor man he is who wants nothing, I reply in this way: So long as a man has this as his will, that he wants to fulfill God's dearest will, he has not the poverty about which we want to talk. Such a person has a will with which he wants to fulfill God's will, and that is not true poverty. For if a person wants really to have poverty, he ought to be as free of his own created will as he was when he did not exist. For I tell you by the truth that is eternal, so long as you have a will to fulfill God's will, and a longing for God and for eternity, then you are not poor; for a poor man is one who has a will and longing for nothing.

When I stood in my first cause, I then had no "God," and then I was my own cause. I wanted nothing, I longed for nothing, for I was an empty being, and the only truth in which I rejoiced was in the knowledge of myself. Then it was myself that I wanted and nothing else. What I wanted I was, and what I was I wanted; and so I stood, empty of God and of everything. But when I went out from my own free will and received my created being, then I had a "God," for before there were any creatures, God was not "God," but he was what he was. But when creatures came to be and received their created being, then God was not "God" in himself, but he was "God" in the creatures.

Now, I say that God, so far as he is "God," is not the perfect end of created beings. The least of these beings possesses in God as much as he possesses. If it could be that a fly had reason and could with its reason seek out the eternal depths of the divine being from which it issued, I say that God, with all that he has as he is "God," could not fulfill or satisfy the fly. So therefore let us pray to God that we may be free of "God," and that we may apprehend and rejoice in that everlasting truth in which the highest angel and the fly and the soul are equal—there where I was established, where I wanted what I was and was what I wanted. So I say: if a man is to become poor in his will, he must want and desire as little as he wanted and desired when he did not exist. And in this way a man is poor who wants nothing.

Next, a man is poor who knows nothing. Sometimes I have said that a man ought to live so that he did not live for himself or for the truth or for God. But now I say something different and something more: that a man who would possess this poverty ought to live as if he does not even know that he is not in any way living for himself or for the truth or for God. Rather, he should be so free of all knowing that he does not know or experience or grasp that God lives in him. For when man was established in God's everlasting being, there was no different life in him. What was living there was himself. So I say that a man should be set as free of his own knowing as he was when he was not. Let God perform what he will, and let man be free.

Everything that ever came from God is directed into pure activity. Now, the actions proper to a man are loving and knowing. The question is: in which of these does blessedness most consist? Some authorities have said that it consists in knowing, others that it consists in loving; others say that it consists in knowing and loving, and what they say is better. But I say that it does not consist in either knowing or loving, but that there is that in the soul from which knowing and loving flow; that something does not know or love as do the powers of the soul. Whoever knows this knows in what blessedness consists. That something has neither before nor after, and it is not waiting for anything that is to come, for it can neither gain nor lose. So it is deprived of the knowledge that God is acting in it; but it is itself the very thing that rejoices in itself as

God does in himself. So I say that a man ought to be established, free and empty, not knowing or perceiving that God is acting in him; and so a man may possess poverty. The authorities say that God is a being, and a rational one, and that he knows all things. I say that God is neither being nor rational, and that he does not know this or that. Therefore God is free of all things, and therefore he is all things. Whoever will be poor in spirit, he must be poor of all his own knowledge, so that he knows nothing—not God or created things or himself. Therefore it is necessary for a man to long not to be able to know or perceive God's works. In this way a man can be poor of his own knowledge.

Third, a man is poor who has nothing. Many people have said that it is perfection when one possesses no material, earthly things, and in one sense this is indeed true, if a man does this voluntarily. But this is not the sense in which I mean it.

I have said just now that a man is poor who does not want to fulfill God's will, but who lives so that he may be free both of his own will and of God's will, as he was when he was not. About this poverty I say that it is the highest poverty. Second, I say that a man is poor who knows nothing of God's works in him. A man who is so established is as free of knowing and perceiving as God is free of all things, and this is the purest poverty. But a third form is the most intimate poverty, on which I now want to speak; and this is when a man has nothing.

Now, pay great attention and give heed! I have often said, and great authorities say, that a man should be so free of all things and of all works, both interior and exterior, that he might become a place only for God, in which God could work. Now, I say otherwise. If it be the case that man is free of all created things and of God and of himself, and if it also be that God may find a place in him in which to work, then I say that as long as that is in man, he is not poor with the most intimate poverty. For it is not God's intention in his works that man should have in himself a place for God to work in. Poverty of spirit is for a man to keep so free of God and of all his works that if God wishes to work in the soul, he himself is the place in which he wants to work; and that he will gladly do. For if he finds a man as poor as this, then God performs his own work, and the man is in this way suffering God to work, and God is his own place to work in, and so God is his own worker in himself. Thus in this poverty man pursues that everlasting being that he was and that he is now and that he will evermore remain.

It is Saint Paul who says: "All that I am, I am by God's grace" (1 Cor 15:10). But if what I say transcends grace and being and understanding and will and longing, how then can Paul's words be true? People show that what Paul said is true in this way: That the grace of God was in him was necessarily so, for it was God's grace working in him that brought what was accidental to the perfection of the essential. When grace had finished and had perfected its work, then Paul remained what he was.

So I say that man should be so poor that he should not be or have any place in which God could work. When man clings to place, he clings to distinction. Therefore I pray to God that he may make me free of "God," for my real being is above God, if we take

"God" to be the beginning of created things. For in the same being of God where God is above being and above distinction, there I myself was; there I willed myself and committed myself to create this man. Therefore I am the cause of myself in the order of my being, which is eternal, and not in the order of my becoming, which is temporal. And therefore I am unborn, and in the manner in which I am unborn I can never die. In my unborn manner I have been eternally, and am now, and shall eternally remain. What I am in the order of having been born—that will die and perish, for it is mortal, and so it must in time suffer corruption. In my birth all things were born and I was the cause of myself and of all things; and if I would have wished it, I would not be, nor would all other things be. And if I did not exist, "God" would also not exist. That God is "God," of that I am a cause; if I did not exist, God, too, would not be "God." There is no need to understand this.

A great authority says that his breaking through is nobler than his flowing out; and that is true. When I flowed out from God, all things said: "God is." And this cannot make me blessed, for with this I acknowledge that I am a creature. But in the breaking through, when I come to be free of will of myself and of God's will and of all his works and of God himself, then I am above all created things, and I am neither God nor creature, but I am what I was and what I shall remain, now and eternally. Then I received an impulse that will bring me up above all the angels. Together with this impulse, I receive such riches that God, as he is "God," and as he performs all his divine works, cannot suffice me; for in this breaking through I receive that God and I are one. Then I am what I was, and then I neither diminish nor increase, for I am then an immovable cause that moves all things. Here God finds no place in man, for with this poverty man achieves what he has been eternally and will evermore remain. Here God is one with the spirit, and that is the most intimate poverty one can find.

Whoever does not understand what I have said, let him not burden his heart with it; for as long as a man is not equal to this truth, he will not understand these words, for this is a truth beyond speculation that has come immediately from the heart of God. May God help us so to live that we may find it eternally. Amen.

Sermon 53

When I preach, I am accustomed to speak about detachment, and that a man should be free of himself and of all things; second, that a man should be formed again into that simple good which is God; third, that he should reflect on the great nobility with which God has endowed his soul, so that in this way he may come to wonder at God; fourth, about the purity of the divine nature, for the brightness of the divine nature is beyond words. God is a word, a word unspoken.

Augustine says: "All writings are in vain. If one says that God is a word, he has been expressed; but if one says that God has not been spoken, he is ineffable." And yet he is something, but who can speak this word? No one can do this, except him who is this Word. God is a Word that speaks itself. Wherever God is, he speaks this Word; wherever he is not, he does not speak. God is spoken and unspoken. The Father is a speaking work, and the Son is speech working. Whatever is in me proceeds from me; if I only think it, my word manifests it, and still it remains in me. So does the Father speak the unspoken Son, and yet the Son remains in him. And I have often said: "God's going out is his going in." To the extent that I am close to God, so to that extent God utters himself into me. The more that all rational creatures in their works go out of themselves, the more they go into themselves. This is not so with merely corporeal creatures; the more they work, the more they go out of themselves. All creatures want to utter God in all their works; they all come as close as they can in uttering him, and yet they cannot utter him. Whether they wish it or not, whether they like it or not, they all want to utter God, and yet he remains unuttered.

David says: "The Lord is his name" (Ps 67:5). Lord signifies being promoted in power, servant means subjection. There are some names that are proper to God and inappropriate to all other things, such as "God." "God" is the name most proper to God of all names, as "man" is the name of men. A man is a man, be he foolish or wise. Seneca says: "That man is a pitiful creature who cannot rise above other men." Some names denote a connection with God, such as "fatherhood" and "sonship." When one says "father," one understands "son." No one can be a father if he does not have a son, nor can a son be a son if he has no father; both of them have an eternal relationship that is beyond time. Third, there are some names that signify a lifting up to God and a regard to

time. In scripture God is called by many names. I say that whoever perceives something in God and attaches thereby some name
to him—that is not God. God is above names and above nature.
We read of one good man who was entreating God in his prayer
and wanted to give names to him. Then a brother said: "Be quiet.
You are dishonoring God." We cannot find a single name we
might give to God. Yet those names are permitted to us by which
the saints have called him and which God so consecrated with
divine light and poured into all their hearts. And through these
we should first learn how we ought to pray to God. We should
say: "Lord, with the same names that you have so consecrated in
the hearts of your saints and have poured into all their hearts, so
we pray to you and praise you." Second, we should learn not to
give any name to God, lest we imagine that in so doing we have
praised and exalted him as we should; for God is "above names"
and ineffable.

The Father speaks the Son out of all his power, and he speaks in
him all things. All created things are God's speech. The being of a
stone speaks and manifests the same as does my mouth about
God; and people understand more by what is done than by what
is said. The work that is performed by the highest nature in its
greatest power is not understood by an inferior nature. If the
inferior nature performed the same work, it would not be subject
to the highest nature; they would be the same. All creatures
would like to echo God in their works, but there is little indeed
they can manifest. Even the highest angels, as they mount toward
and touch God, are as unlike that which is in God as white is

unlike black. What all creatures have received is quite unlike him, except only that they would gladly express him as closely as they can. The prophet says: "Lord, you say one thing, and I hear two things" (Ps 61:12). As God speaks into the soul, the soul and he are one; but as soon as this goes, there is a separation. The more that we ascend in our understanding, the more are we one in him. Therefore the Father speaks the Son always, in unity, and pours out in him all created things. They are all called to return into whence they have flowed out. All their life and their being is a calling and a hastening back to him from whom they have issued.

The prophet says: "The Lord stretched out his hand" (Jer 1:9), and he means the Holy Spirit. Now, he says: "He has touched my mouth," and goes on at once, "and has spoken to me." The soul's mouth is its highest part, which the soul means when it says: "He has put his word in my mouth" (Jer 1:9). That is the kiss of the soul, there mouth touches mouth, there the Father bears his Son into the soul, and there the soul is spoken to. Now, he says: "Take heed; today I have chosen you, and have placed you above peoples and above kingdoms" (Jer 1:10). In a "today" God vows that he will choose us where there is nothing, and where yet in an eternity there is a "today." "And I have placed you above peoples"—that is, above all the world, of which you must be free—"and above kingdoms"—that is, whatever is more than one, which is too much, for you must die to all things and be formed again into the heights, where we dwell in the Holy Spirit.

May God the Holy Spirit help us to that end. Amen.

Sermon 83

"Be renewed in your spirit" (Eph 4:23), which is here called *mens*—that is, your disposition. This is what Saint Paul says.

Augustine says that in the highest part of the soul, which he calls *mens*, or disposition, God created together with the soul's being a power, which the authorities call a store or a coffer of spiritual forms or formal images. This power makes the soul resemble the Father in his outflowing divinity, out of which he has poured the whole treasure of his divine being into the Son and into the Holy Spirit, differentiating between the Persons, just as the soul's memory pours the treasure of its images into the soul's powers. So when the soul with these powers contemplates what consists of images, whether that be an angel's image or its own, there is for the soul something lacking. Even if the soul contemplates God, either as God or as an image or as three, the soul lacks something. But if all images are detached from the soul, and it contemplates only the simple One, then the soul's naked being finds the naked, formless being of the divine unity, which is there a being above being, accepting and reposing in itself. Ah, marvel of marvels, how noble is that acceptance, when the soul's being can accept nothing other than the naked unity of God!

Now, Saint Paul says: "Be renewed in the spirit." Renewal happens to all created beings under God; but no renewal comes to God, but evermore only eternity. What is eternity? Pay heed! It is the property of eternity that in it being and youth are one because eternity would not be eternal if it could be renewed, if it did not always exist. So I say: Renewal happens to the angels, as the future is intimated to them, for an angel knows about future things, though only so much as God reveals to him. And renewal happens also to the soul, so far as "soul" is its name, for it is called *soul* because it gives life to the body and is a form of the body. To a soul, too, renewal happens, so far as "spirit" is its name. It is called *spirit* because it is detached from here and now and from the whole natural order. But when it is an image of God and as nameless as God, then no renewal happens to it, but only eternity, as in God.

Now, pay attention: God is nameless, because no one can say anything or understand anything about him. Therefore a pagan teacher says: "Whatever we understand or say about the First Cause, that is far more ourselves than it is the First Cause, for it is beyond all saying and understanding." So if I say: "God is good," that is not true. I am good, but God is not good. I can even say: "I am better than God," for whatever is good can become better, and whatever can become better can become best of all. But since God is not good, he cannot become better. And since he cannot become better, he cannot be best of all. For these three degrees are alien to God—"good," "better," and "best"—for he is superior to them all. And if I say: "God is wise," that is not true. I am wiser than he. If I say: "God is a being," it is not true; he is a being transcending being and a transcending nothingness. About this, Saint Augustine says: "The best that one can say about God is for one to keep silent out of the wisdom of one's inward riches." So be silent, and do not chatter about God; for when you do chatter about him, you are telling lies and sinning. But if you want to be without sin and perfect, you should not chatter about God. And do not try to understand God, for God is beyond all understanding. One authority says: "If I had a God whom I could understand, I should never consider him God." If you can understand anything about him, it in no way belongs to him, and insofar as you understand anything about him, that brings you into incomprehension, and from incomprehension you arrive at a brute's stupidity; for when created beings do not understand, they resemble the brutes. So if you do not wish to be brutish, do not understand the God who is beyond words. "Then what ought I to do?" You ought to sink down out of all your your-ness, and flow into his his-ness, and your "yours" and his "his" ought to become one "mine," so completely that you with him perceive forever his uncreated is-ness, and his nothingness, for which there is no name.

Now, Saint Paul says: "You should be renewed in the spirit." If we want to be renewed in the spirit, each of the soul's six powers, the superior and the inferior powers, must have a ring of gold, gilded with the gold of divine love. Now, pay heed! There are three inferior powers: The first is called *rational*, and it is discretion, and on it you ought to wear a golden ring, which is the light, a divine light, with which your powers of discretion should always be illumined. The next is called *irascible*, the "angry power," and on it you ought to have a ring, which is your peace. "Why?" Because as much as you are at peace, so much are you in God, and as much as you lack peace, so much do you lack God. The third power is called *appetitive*, and on it you ought to wear a ring,

which is contentment; that is, you should be content with all
creatures who are under God, but you should never be content
with God, because you can never be content with God. The more
you have of God, the more you long for him, for if you could be
content with God, and such a contentment with him were to
come, God would not be God.

And you must also wear a golden ring on each of the superior
powers. There are, too, three superior powers: The first is called a
retentive power, *memory*. This power one compares with the Father
in the Trinity, and on it you should have a golden ring—that is, a
retention so that you hold on to everything that is eternal. The
second power is called *intellectual*, understanding. This power one
compares with the Son, and you ought to wear on it a golden
ring—that is, an understanding so that you should always perceive God. "And how?" You should perceive him without images,
without a medium, and without comparisons. But if I am to perceive God so, without a medium, then I must just become him,
and he must become me. I say more: God must just become me,
and I must just become God, so completely one that this "he" and
this "I" become and are one "is" and, in this is-ness, eternally
perform one work, for this "he," who is God, and this "I," which
is the soul, are greatly fruitful. But let there be a single "here" or a
single "now," and the "I" and the "he" will never perform anything or become one. The third power is called *voluntary*, the will,
and one compares it with the Holy Spirit. On it you should wear
a golden ring—that is, love. You should love God. You should love
God apart from his lovableness—that is, not because he is lovable,

for God is unlovable. He is above all love and lovableness. "Then how should I love God?" You should love God unspiritually; that is, your soul should be unspiritual and stripped of all spirituality, for as long as your soul has a spirit's form, it has images, and as long as it has images, it has a medium, and as long as it has a medium, it has not unity or simplicity. Therefore your soul must be unspiritual, free of all spirit, and must remain spiritless; for if you love God as he is God, as he is spirit, as he is person, and as he is image—all this must go! "Then how should I love him?" You should love him as he is a non-God, a nonspirit, a nonperson, a nonimage, but as he is a pure, unmixed, bright "One," separated from all duality; and in that One we should eternally sink down, out of "something" into "nothing."

May God help us to that. Amen.

ON DETACHMENT

I have read many writings both by the pagan teachers and by the prophets, and in the Old and the New Law, and I have inquired, carefully and most industriously, to find which is the greatest and best virtue with which man can most completely and closely conform himself to God, with which he can by grace become that which God is by nature, and with which man can come most of all to resemble that image which he was in God, and between which and God there was no distinction before ever God made created things. And as I scrutinize all these writings, as far as my reason can lead and instruct me, I find no other virtue better than a pure detachment from all things; because all other virtues have some regard for created things, but detachment is free from all created things. That is why our Lord said to Martha: "One thing is necessary" (Lk 10:42), which is as much as to say: "Martha, whoever wants to be free of care and to be pure must have one thing, and that is detachment."

The teachers have great things to say in praise of love, as had Saint Paul, who says: "Whatever I may practice, if I do not have love, I am worth nothing at all" (1 Cor 13:1–2). And yet I praise detachment above all love. First, because the best thing about love is that it compels me to love God, yet detachment compels God to love me. Now, it is far greater for me to compel God to come to me than to compel myself to come to God; and that is because God is able to conform himself, far better and with more suppleness, and to unite himself with me than I could unite myself with God. And I prove that detachment compels God to come to me in this way: It is because everything longs to achieve its own natural place. Now, God's own natural place is unity and purity, and that comes from detachment. Therefore God must of necessity give himself to a heart that has detachment. Second, I praise detachment above love because love compels me to suffer all things for God's love, yet detachment leads me to where I am receptive to nothing except God. Now, it is far greater to be receptive to nothing except God than to suffer all things for God's love, for man when he suffers has some regard for the created things from which he receives the suffering, but detachment is wholly free of all created things. And that detachment is receptive to nothing at all except God. That I prove in this way: Whatever is to be received must be received by something; but detachment is so close to nothingness that there is nothing so subtle that it can be apprehended by detachment, except God alone. He is so simple and so subtle that he can indeed be apprehended in a detached heart. And so detachment can apprehend nothing except God.

The authorities also praise humility above many other virtues. But I praise detachment above all humility, and that is because, although there may be humility without detachment, there cannot be perfect detachment without perfect humility, because perfect humility proceeds from annihilation of self. Now, detachment approaches so closely to nothingness that there can be nothing between perfect detachment and nothingness. Therefore perfect detachment cannot exist without humility. Now, two virtues are always better than one. The second reason I praise detachment above humility is that perfect humility is always abasing itself below all created things, and in this abasement man goes out of himself toward created things; but detachment remains within itself. Now, there can never be any going out of self so excellent that remaining within self is not itself much more excellent. The prophet David said of this: "All the glory of the king's daughter is from her inwardness." Perfect detachment has no looking up to, no abasement—not beneath any created thing or above it. It wishes to be neither beneath nor above; it wants to exist by itself, not giving joy or sorrow to anyone, not wanting equality or inequality with any created thing, not wishing for this or wishing for that. All that it wants is to be. But to wish to be this thing or that—this it does not want. Whoever wants to be this or that wants to be something, but detachment wants to be nothing at all. So it is that detachment makes no claim upon anything.

Now, a man could say: "All virtues were most perfectly present in our Lady, so that she must have had perfect detachment." But if detachment is more excellent than humility, why did our Lady single out not her detachment but her humility when she said: "Because he has regarded the humility of his handmaid" (Lk 1:48)? Why did she not say: "He has regarded the detachment of his handmaid?" To this I answer and say that detachment and humility are in God, as far as we can speak of virtues as present in God. Now, you must know that it was loving humility that brought God to abase himself into human nature; yet when he became man, detachment remained immovable in itself as it was when he created the kingdoms of heaven and earth, as afterward I intend to say to you. And when our Lord, wishing to become man, remained immovable in his detachment, our Lady knew well that this was what he desired also from her, and that on that account it was to her humility that he was looking, not to her detachment. So she remained immovable in her detachment, and praised in herself not detachment but humility. And if she had by so much as a word mentioned her detachment, and had said: "He has regarded my detachment," detachment would have been troubled by that, and would not have remained wholly perfect, for there would then have been a going out. There can be no going out, however small, in which detachment can remain unblemished. And so you have the reason our Lady singled out her humility and not her detachment. The prophet spoke about that: "I shall hear what the Lord God will say in me" (Ps 84:9)— that is, I shall be silent and hear what my God and my Lord may say in me, as if he were to say: "If God wishes to speak to me, let him come in here to me; I do not want to go out."

I also praise detachment above all mercifulness, because mercifulness is nothing other than man's going out of himself to the shortcomings of his fellow men, and through this his heart becomes troubled. But detachment remains free of this, and remains in itself, and allows nothing to trouble it, for nothing can ever trouble a man unless things are not well with him. In a few words: if I regard all virtues, I find not one so much without shortcomings and so leading us to God as detachment.

An authority called Avicenna says: "The excellence of the spirit that has achieved detachment is so great that whatever it contemplates is true, and whatever it desires is granted, and whatever it commands one must obey." And you should know that this is really so; when the free spirit has attained true detachment, it compels God to its being; and if the spirit could attain formlessness, and be without all accidents, it would take on God's properties. But this God can give to no one but to himself; therefore God cannot do more for the spirit that has attained detachment than to give himself to it. And the man who has attained this complete detachment is so carried into eternity that no transient thing can move him, so that he experiences nothing of whatever is bodily, and he calls the world dead, because nothing earthly has any savor for him. This is what Saint Paul meant when he said: "I live, and yet I do not; Christ lives in me" (Gal 2:20).

Now, you may ask what detachment is since it is in itself so excellent. Here you should know that true detachment is nothing other than for the spirit to stand as immovable against whatever may chance to it of joy and sorrow, honor, shame, and disgrace, as a mountain of lead stands before a little breath of wind. This immovable detachment brings a man into the greatest equality with God, because God has it from his immovable detachment that he is God, and it is from his detachment that he has his purity and his simplicity and his unchangeability. And if man is to become equal with God, insofar as a creature can have equality with God, that must happen through detachment. It then draws a man into purity, and from purity into simplicity, and from simplicity into unchangeability, and these things produce an equality between God and the man; and the equality must come about in grace, for it is grace that draws a man away from all temporal things, and makes him pure from all transient things. And you must know that to be empty of all created things is to be full of God, and to be full of created things is to be empty of God.

Now, you must know that God has been in this immovable detachment since before the world began, and he still remains so; and you must know that when God created heaven and earth and all created things, that affected his immovable detachment as little as if no creature had ever been made. And I say more: all the prayers and good works that man can accomplish in time move God's detachment as little as if no single prayer or good work were ever performed in time, and yet for this God is never any less gentle or less inclined toward man than if he had never achieved prayer or good works. And I say more: when the Son in his divinity wished to become man, and became man, and suffered his passion, that affected God's immovable detachment as little as if the Son had never become man. Now, you may say: "If I hear rightly, all prayers and good works are wasted, because God does not accept them in such a way that anyone could move him through them; and yet people say that God wants to be asked for everything." But here you must pay me good attention, and understand properly, if you can, that God, in his first everlasting glance—if we can think of his first glancing at anything—saw all things as they were to happen, and in that same glance he saw when and how he would make all created things, and when the Son would become man and would suffer. He also saw the smallest prayer and good work that anyone would ever perform, and he took into his regard which prayers and devotion he would or should give ear to. He saw what you will earnestly pray and entreat him for tomorrow; and it will not be tomorrow that he will give ear to your entreaty and prayer, because he has heard it in his everlastingness, before ever you became man. But if your prayer is not insistent and lacks earnestness, it will not be now that God refuses you, because he has refused you in his everlastingness. And so God has looked upon all things in his first everlasting glance, and God does not undertake anything whatever afresh, because everything is something already accomplished. And so God always remains in his immovable detachment, and yet men's prayers and good works are not on this account wasted; for whoever does well will also be well rewarded; whoever does evil will be rewarded accordingly. This is the meaning of what Saint Augustine says in the fifth book of On the Trinity, in the last chapter, where he begins: "Yet God . . . ," which has this sense:

God forbid that anyone should say that God loves anyone in time, because with him nothing is past, and nothing is to come, and he had loved all the saints before ever the world was created, when he foresaw that they would be. And when it comes to pass in time that he in time regards what he has looked upon in eternity, then people think that God has turned to them with a new love; yet it is so that whether God be angry or confer some blessing, it is we who are changed, and he remains unchangeable, as the light of the sun is painful to sick eyes and good for healthy ones, and yet the light of the sun remains in itself unchangeable.

And he touches on the same meaning in the twelfth book of On the Trinity, in the fourth chapter, where he says: "God does not

see in temporal fashion, and nothing new happens in his sight."
Isidore also means this, in his book about the highest good,
where he says: "Many people ask what God did before he created
heaven and earth, or when the new will in God to make created
things came about." He answers this so: "No new will ever came
about in God, because when it was so that the creature was in
itself nothing"—of what it now is—"still it was before the world
began, in God and in his mind." God did not create heaven and
earth in the temporal fashion in which we describe it—"Let there
be!"—because all created things were spoken in the everlasting
Word. We must also deduce this from the Lord's colloquy with
Moses, when Moses said to the Lord: "Lord, if Pharaoh asks me
who you are, what shall I say to him?" and the Lord said: "Say, 'He
who is has sent me'" (Ex 3:10–14), which is as much as to say:
he who is in himself unchangeable—he has sent me.

Now, someone might say: "Did Christ have immovable detachment, even when he said, 'My soul is sorrowful even to death'
(Mt 26:38), and did Mary, when she stood beneath the cross?—
and people tell us much about her lamentations. How can all this
be reconciled with immovable detachment?" Here you must
know that the authorities say that in every man there are two
kinds of man: One is called the outer man, which is the man's
sensuality, with the five senses serving him, and yet the outer
man works through the power of the soul. The second man is
called the inner man, which is the man's inwardness. Now, you
should know that a spiritual man who loves God makes no use in
his outer man of the soul's powers except when the five senses

require it; and his inwardness pays no heed to the five senses, except as this leads and guides them, and protects them, so that they are not employed for beastly purposes, as they are by some people who live for their carnal delight, as beasts lacking reason do. Such people deserve to be called beasts rather than men. And whatever power the soul possesses, beyond that which it gives to the five senses, it gives wholly to the inner man, and if he has a high and noble object, the soul draws to itself all its powers it had loaned to the five senses. Then the man is called senseless and rapt, for his object is an image that the reason can apprehend, or, it may be, something reasonable that has no image. Yet know that God requires every spiritual man to love him with all the powers of his soul. Of this he said: "Love your God with your whole heart" (Dt 6:5). But there are people who squander all the soul's powers on the outer man. They are those who apply all their intelligence and reason to perishable goods, and who know nothing about the inner man. Now, you must know that the outer man may be active while the inner man remains wholly free and immovable. In Christ, too, there was an outer man and an inner man, and also in our Lady; and whatever Christ and our Lady may have said about outward affairs, they acted according to the outer man, and the inner man remained in an immovable detachment. And Christ spoke in this sense when he said: "My soul is sorrowful even to death"; and however much our Lady lamented, and whatever else she may have said, still always her inwardness remained in an immovable detachment. Consider a simile of this: a door, opening and shutting on a hinge. I compare the planks on the outside of the door with the outer man, but the hinge with the inner man. As the door opens and shuts, the outside planks move backward and forward, but the hinge remains immovable in one place, and the opening and shutting do not affect it. It is just the same here, if you can understand it rightly.

And now I ask: "What is the object of this pure detachment?" My answer is that neither this nor that is the object of pure detachment. It reposes in a naked nothingness, and I shall tell you why that is: Pure detachment reposes in the highest place. If a man has repose in the highest place, God can work in him according to his whole will. But God cannot work according to his whole will in every man's heart, for though it may be that God is omnipotent, still he cannot work except where he finds or creates a willing cooperation. And I say "or creates" because of Saint Paul, for in him God did not find willing cooperation, but he made Paul willing by the inpouring of grace. So I say: God works according as he finds willingness. He works in one way in men, and another in stones. We can find an analogy of this in nature: If someone heats a baker's oven, and puts in one loaf of oats and another of rye and another of wheat, there is only one temperature in the oven, but it does not have the same effect upon the different doughs, because one turns into fine bread, another is coarse, and a third even coarser. And that is not the fault of the temperature but of the materials, which are not the same. In the same way, God does not work alike in every man's heart; he works as he finds willingness and receptivity. There may be one thing or another in some heart, on which one thing or another God cannot work to bring it up to the highest place. And if the heart is to be willing for that highest place, it must repose in a naked nothingness; and in this there is the greatest potentiality that can be. And when the heart that has detachment attains to the highest place, that must be nothingness, for in this is the greatest receptivity. See an analogy of this in nature: If I want to write on a wax tablet, it does not matter how fine the words may be that are written on the tablet; they still hinder me from writing on it. If I really want to write something, I must erase and eliminate everything that is already there; and the tablet is never so good for me to write on as when there is nothing on it at all. In the same way, if God is to write on my heart up in the highest place, everything that can be called this or that must come out of my heart, and in that way my heart will have won detachment. And so God can work upon it in the highest place and according to his highest will. And this is why the heart in its detachment has no this or that as its object.

But now I ask: "What is the prayer of a heart that has detachment?" And to answer it I say that purity in detachment does not know how to pray, because if someone prays he asks God to get something for him, or he asks God to take something away from him. But a heart in detachment asks for nothing, nor has it anything of which it would gladly be free. So it is free of all prayer, and its prayer is nothing other than for uniformity with God. That is all its prayer consists in. To illustrate this meaning we may consider what Saint Dionysius said about Saint Paul's words, when he said: "There are many of you racing for the crown, but it will be

given only to one" (1 Cor 9:24): all the powers of the soul are racing for the crown, but it will be given only to the soul's being. And
Dionysius says: "The race is nothing but a turning away from all
created things and a uniting oneself with that which is uncreated."
And as the soul attains this, it loses its name and it draws God into
itself, so that in itself it becomes nothing, as the sun draws up the
red dawn into itself so that it becomes nothing. Nothing else will
bring man to this except pure detachment. And we can also apply
to this what Augustine says: "The soul has a secret entry into the
divine nature when all things become nothing to it." This entry
here on this earth is nothing other than pure detachment. And
when this detachment ascends to the highest place, it knows nothing of knowing, it loves nothing of loving, and from light it
becomes dark. To this we can also apply what one teacher says:
"The poor in spirit are those who have abandoned all things for
God, just as they were his when we did not exist." No one can do
this but a heart with pure detachment. We can see that God would
rather be in a heart with such detachment than in all hearts. For if
you ask me: "What is it God seeks in all things?" then I answer
you out of the book of Wisdom, where he says: "In all things I
seek rest" (Sir 14:11). Nowhere is there complete rest, except only
in the heart that has found detachment. Hence God would rather
be there than in other virtues or in any other things. And you
should also know that the more a man applies himself to becoming susceptible to the divine inflowing, the more blessed will he
be; and whoever can establish himself in the highest readiness, he
will also be in the highest blessedness. Now, no one can make

himself susceptible to the divine inflowing except through uniformity with God, for as each man becomes uniform with God, to
that measure he becomes susceptible to the divine inflowing. And
uniformity comes from man's subjecting himself to God; and the
more a man subjects himself to created things, the less is he uniform with God. Now, a heart that has pure detachment is free of
all created things, and so it is wholly submitted to God, and so it
achieves the highest uniformity with God, and is most susceptible
to the divine inflowing. This is what Saint Paul means when he
says: "Put on Jesus Christ" (Rom 13:14). He means through uniformity with Christ, and this putting on cannot happen except
through uniformity with Christ. And you must know that when
Christ became man, it was not just a human being he put on himself; he put on human nature. Therefore do you, too, go out of all
things, and then there will be only what Christ accepted and put
on, and so you will have put on Christ.

Whoever now wishes to see properly what is the excellence
and the profit of perfect detachment, let him take good heed of
Christ's words when he spoke about his human nature and said to
his disciples: "It is expedient for you that I go from you, for if I
do not go, the Holy Spirit cannot come to you" (Jn 16:7). This is
just as if he were to say: "You have taken too much delight in my
present image, so that the perfect delight of the Holy Spirit cannot be yours. So detach yourselves from the image, and unite
yourselves to the formless being, for God's spiritual consolation is
delicate; therefore he will not offer it to anyone except to him
who disdains bodily consolations."

Now, all you reasonable people, take heed! No one is happier than a man who has attained the greatest detachment. No one can accept fleshly and bodily consolations without spiritual damage, "because the flesh longs in opposition to the spirit and the spirit to the flesh" (Gal 5:17). Therefore whoever sows in the flesh inordinate love will reap everlasting death, and whoever in the spirit sows a well-ordered love will from the spirit reap everlasting life (Gal 6:8). So it is that the sooner a man shuns what is created, the sooner will the creator come to him. So take heed, all you reasonable people! Since the delight we might have in Christ's bodily image deprives us of receptivity for the Holy Spirit, how much more shall we be deprived of God by the ill-ordered delight that we take in transient consolations! So detachment is the best of all, for it purifies the soul and cleanses the conscience and enkindles the heart and awakens the spirit and stimulates our longings and shows us where God is and separates us from created things and unites itself with God.

Now, all you reasonable people, take heed! The fastest beast that will carry you to your perfection is suffering, for no one will enjoy more eternal sweetness than those who endure with Christ in the greatest bitterness. There is nothing more gall-bitter than suffering, and nothing more honey-sweet than to have suffered; nothing disfigures the body more than suffering, and nothing more adorns the soul in the sight of God than to have suffered. The firmest foundation on which this perfection can stand is humility, for whichever mortal crawls here in the deepest abasement, his spirit will fly up into the highest realms of the divinity, for love brings sorrow, and sorrow brings love. And therefore, whoever longs to attain to perfect detachment, let him struggle for perfect humility, and so he will come close to the divinity.

That we may all be brought to this, may that supreme detachment help us that is God himself. Amen.

THE BOOK OF DIVINE CONSOLATION, FROM THE BOOK OF "BENEDICTUS"

Benedictus deus et pater domini nostri iesu christi

(2 Cor 1:3).

The noble apostle Saint Paul says these words: "Blessed be the God and Father of our Lord Jesus Christ, a Father of mercy and God of all comfort, who comforts us in all our tribulations" (2 Cor 1:3). There are three kinds of tribulation that touch and oppress a man in this sorrowful life. One is the harm that may come to his material possessions. The second is what may happen to his kinsfolk and his friends. The third is what may happen to him: disgraces and sufferings, the pains of his body, and the sorrows of his heart.

That is why I want in this book to write some counsels with which a man can console himself in all his sufferings, afflictions, and sorrow; and the book has three parts. In the first he will find various true sayings, and in them he will find the ready and complete comfort he ought to have for all his sorrows. Then next there are some thirty topics and precepts, from each of which he can always gain great consolation. Then in the third part of the book he will find examples of what wise men have done and have said when they were suffering.

Part 2

Here now in the second part are some thirty topics, each of which ought readily to console a rational man in his sorrow.

The first is that there is no affliction and harm that is without consolation, nor is there any harm that is nothing but harm. That is why Saint Paul says that God's faithfulness and goodness do not suffer any temptation or sorrow to become unendurable (1 Cor 10:15). He always makes and gives some comfort with which a man can help himself; for the saints and the pagan philosophers also say that God and nature do not permit unmixed evil or suffering to exist.

I give you an example: A man has a hundred marks, of which he loses forty and retains sixty. If he is going to think day and night about the forty he has lost, he will never stop feeling aggrieved and sorry for himself. How could anyone find consolation and forget his sorrow who keeps coming back to his loss and his grief, thinking about what it has done to him and what he has become through it, staring at affliction while affliction stares back at him, moaning over it while it moans in reply, as they sit there, affliction and he, gazing into each other's eyes? But if he would just turn his mind to the sixty marks he still has, and turn his back on the forty that are lost, and think of what the sixty are to him, and if he would look at them face-to-face and chat with them, he would certainly find consolation. What exists and what is good can console me; but what is nonexistent and is not good, what is not mine and what I have lost—that must of necessity bring desolation and sorrow and affliction. Solomon says about this: "In the day of evils do not be unmindful of the day of good things" (Sir 11:27). That is to say: when you are in sorrow and affliction, think of the good things and the comfort you still have and possess. And it ought to console a man if he will think how many thousands of people there are who, if they had the sixty marks he still has, would consider themselves fine ladies and gentlemen, and that they were very rich, and would be glad of heart.

But there is something else that should console a man. If he is sick and in great bodily pain, he still has a house and what he needs to eat and drink, doctors to treat him, his servants to look after him, his friends to sympathize and be with him. What more does he want? What do poor people do when they have times when they are as sick or even sicker, and have no one to give them a cup of cold water? They have to go out begging a crust of bread in the rain and the snow and the cold, from house to house. So if you want consolation, forget those who are better off and think of all those for whom things are worse.

What is more, I say this: all sorrow comes from love and from holding dear. Therefore, if I feel sorrow because of perishable things, my heart and I will still love and hold dear perishable things, and God still does not have the love of my whole heart, and I still do not love such things as God would have me love with him. Is it then any wonder that God decrees that I so justly suffer harm and sorrow?

Saint Augustine says: "Lord, I did not want to lose you, but I wanted to possess, along with you, the created things that I crave; and that is why I lost you—because you do not want anyone to possess, along with you who are the truth, the falsehood and deceits of created things." And in another place he says: "The man who is not content with God alone is too greedy by far." And somewhere else he says: "How could God's gifts to his creatures content a man who is not content with God himself?" Everything that is alien to God, and that is not God himself alone, ought to be for a good man not consolation but a torment. He ought always to say: "Lord, my God and my comfort, if you turn me away from yourself to anything, give me another you, so that I pass from you to you, for I want nothing except you." When the Lord promised Moses everything that is good and sent him into the Holy Land, which signifies the kingdom of heaven, Moses said: "Lord, do not send me anywhere if you are not willing to come with me yourself" (Ex 33:15).

All attraction and desire and love come from that which is like, because all things are attracted by and love what is like them. The pure man loves everything that is pure, the just man loves and is attracted to justice; a man's lips speak the things that are in the man, as our Lord says: "Out of the abundance of the heart the mouth speaks" (Lk 6:45); and Solomon says: "All the labor of man is in his mouth" (Ec 6:7). Therefore it is a true sign that not God but created things are in a man's heart when he is still attracted and consoled by what is outside him.

This is why a good man ought to feel great shame before God and in his own eyes if he is made aware that God is not within him and that it is not God the Father who is performing his works in him, but that miserable creatures still live in him and attract him and perform his works in him. That is why King David in the Psalms says and laments: "My tears have been my comfort day and night; all the time, men could still say to me:

'Where is your God?'" (Ps 41:4). For to be attracted by external things and to find consolation in what is desolation and to take delight in much talk about it is a true sign that God does not appear in me, does not watch over me, does not work in me. And what is more, a good man should feel shame before good men, that they should detect this in him. He should never complain about his harm and griefs; all that he ought to complain about is that he does complain, and that he is aware of complaint and grief in himself.

The teachers say that under the sky there is a great fire, far and wide, immediate and powerful in its heat, and yet the sky is never affected by it at all. Now, one treatise says that the lowest part of the soul is finer than the highest heaven. How then can a man misjudge himself, thinking that he is a heavenly being with his heart in heaven, if he can still be oppressed and suffer about such little things?

Now, I shall say something else: there can be no good man who does not will what is the particular will of God, for it is impossible for God to will anything but good; and precisely because it is God's will, it becomes and necessarily is good; and what is more, it is the best. And that is why our Lord taught the apostles, and us through them, that we should pray every day for God's will to be done (Mt 6:10). And all the same, when God's will comes to pass and is achieved, then we complain.

Seneca, a pagan philosopher, asks: "What is the best consolation in sorrow and in misfortune?" And he says: "It is for a man to accept everything as if he had wished for it and had asked for it; for you would have wished for it if you had known that everything happens by God's will, with his will, and in his will." A pagan philosopher says: "Leader and commander, Father and Lord of high heaven, I am ready for everything that is your will; give me the will to will according to your will."

A good man ought to have trust and faith and certainty in God, and know him to be so good that it would be impossible to him and to his goodness and to his love to suffer any sorrow or harm to come to a man, unless he should wish to take a greater harm away from him, or to give him greater consolation on earth, or, using the harm as instrument and material, to make something better with it, so that God's glory becomes more widely and more deeply revealed. But, however this may be, in that alone—that it is God's will that it should happen so—a good man's will ought to be so wholly one and united with God's will that he and God have only one will, though that should be for the man's harm or even for his damnation. This is why Saint Paul wished that he might be separated from God, for the love of God, by the will of God, and to the glory of God (Rom 9:3). For a truly perfect man should be accustomed to regard himself as dead, and his self as transformed in God, and so supernaturally changed in God's will that all his blessedness consists in knowing nothing of himself or of anything, and in knowing God alone, in willing and wanting to know nothing but God's will, and in wanting to know God as God knows him, as Saint Paul says (1 Cor 13:12). God knows everything that he knows, he loves and wills everything that he loves and wills, in himself in his own will. Our Lord himself says: "This is eternal life, to know God alone" (Jn 17:3).

This is why the teachers say that the blessed in heaven perceive creatures free from every creaturely image, and that they perceive them in that one image that is God, and in which God knows and loves and wills himself and all things. And that is what God himself teaches us to pray and long for, when we say: "Our Father . . . hallowed be your name"—that is, let us know you alone; "your kingdom come"—that is, that I may possess nothing that I regard as riches except only you who are rich. The Gospel says about this: "Blessed are the poor in spirit" (Mt 5:3)—that is, in the will; and we pray to God that "his will be done on earth"—that is, in us—"as it is in heaven"—that is, in God himself. Such a man is so much of one will with God that he wills everything that God wills, and in the fashion in which God wills it. And therefore, because in some way or other it is God's will that I should have sinned, I should not want not to have done so, for in this way God's will is done "on earth"—that is, in misdeeds—"as it is in heaven"—that is, in good deeds. Thus a man wishes to be deprived of God for God's own sake and for God's own sake to be separated from God, and that alone is true repentance for his sins. And so my sins are to me a painless pain, just as God suffers all wickedness without suffering. I do suffer, and I suffer as much as I can, over sin, because I would not commit a sin for the sake of everything that has been or could be created, even if a thousand worlds could exist forevermore; but I suffer without suffering. And I take and draw the suffering in God's will and from God's will. Only such sorrow is perfect sorrow, because it proceeds and springs from a pure love of God's purest goodness and joy. So it is made true, and men come to know, as I have said in this little book, that the good man, insofar as he is good, becomes possessed of all the properties of goodness itself, which God is in himself.

Now, see what a wonderful and joyful life man has, "on earth as it is in heaven," in God himself. Misfortune serves him as if it were good fortune, and sorrow as much as joy. And see, too, that there is in this a special consolation, for if I have the grace and the goodness of which I have now spoken, I shall always be completely consoled and joyful, at all times and under all circumstances; and if I do not have this, I ought to do without it for the love of God and in his will. If God wills to give what I ask for, I thereby have it and rejoice; and if God does not will to give it, let me accept that I lack it in that same will of God, for this is something that is not his will. And so I obtain, not by obtaining but by lacking. For what is it that I then lack? And truly, man obtains God more truly in lacking than in obtaining; for when a man receives something, the gift possesses in itself that by which he is glad and comforted. But if he does not receive it, he does not have, he does not find, he does not know any cause for joy except God and God's will alone.

But then there is another consolation. If a man has lost some material possession, or a friend or a kinsman, an eye, a hand, or whatever it may be, then he should be sure that if he accepts this patiently for the love of God, then by the loss he did not want to suffer he has in God's reckoning gained at least as much. Suppose that a man loses an eye; he would not for a thousand marks or six thousand marks or more wish to be without the eye. Certainly in God's sight and in God he has saved up for him at least as much as he did not want to lose through such a harm or sorrow. And perhaps this is what is meant when our Lord said: "It is better for you to enter into everlasting life having one eye than to have two eyes and to be lost" (Mt 18:9). It is perhaps also what is meant when God said: "Everyone who has left father and mother, sister and brother, house or land or whatever it may be, will receive a hundredfold, and life everlasting" (Mt 19:29). I am sure that I can say in God's truth, and as I hope to be blessed, that whoever for the love of God and goodness leaves father and mother, brother and sister—or whatever it may be—he receives a hundredfold in two different ways. One is that his father, mother, brother, and sister will become a hundred times dearer to him than they now are. The second way is that not only a hundred people but all people, to the extent that they are people and human beings, will become far dearer to him than his father, mother, or brother now are by his natural inclinations. A man is not aware of this, simply and solely because he has not yet forsaken father and mother, sister and brother, and everything else, purely and only for the love of God and goodness. How has a man left father and mother, sister and brother for the love of God, who still here on earth finds them occupying his heart, who still becomes oppressed and thinks and searches after that which is not God? How has he forsaken everything for the love of God who still is caring and seeking for one good thing or another? Saint Augustine says: "Get rid of these and those goods, and what will remain is pure goodness, moving in its own bare and limitless orbit, and that is God." For as I have already said, goods of any sort do not add anything to goodness, but they conceal and hide the goodness in us. Anyone who sees and contemplates in the light of truth knows and perceives that this is so, because it is true in truth and therefore one must perceive it there and nowhere else.

Yet one should know that possessing virtues and willingness to suffer exist in a wide variety of degrees, just as we can see in nature that one man is bigger and finer than another in stature, in complexion, in knowledge, and in accomplishments. And so I say, too, that a good man may well be good and still be moved and swayed by his natural love for his father, mother, sister, brother—sometimes less, sometimes more—and yet not be wanting in his love for God and for goodness. Yet he becomes good and better in the measure, small or great, to which he is consoled and touched by and is conscious of his natural love for and attraction to his father and mother, sister and brother, and himself.

Yet even so, as I have already written, if a man could accept this as being in God's will—insofar as it is God's will—that human nature should have these deficiencies, through God's particular justice, as a consequence of the sin of the first man, and also, even if that were not so, if he would gladly accept it as God's will for him that he should renounce such natural love, everything would then be well with him, and he would certainly find consolation for his sorrows. That is what is meant when Saint John says that the true "light shines in darkness" (Jn 1:5) and Saint Paul says that "virtue is made perfect in infirmity" (2 Cor 12:9). If a thief were able to suffer death with a true, complete, pure, glad, willing, and joyful love of divine justice, in which and according to which God and his justice will that the evildoer be put to death, truly he would be saved and blessed.

But another consolation is that probably one will find no one who does not love some living person so dearly that he would not gladly sacrifice an eye or go blind for a year, provided that he could have the eye back again, if in this way he could save his friend from death. So if a man would sacrifice his eye for a year, to save from death someone who must still die in a few years' time, he ought rightly and more gladly to sacrifice the ten or twenty or thirty years he might still have to live so as to make himself eternally blessed, possessing the everlasting vision of God in his divine light, seeing, in God, himself and all created beings.

But there is a further consolation: To a good man, insofar as he is good and born of goodness alone and an image of goodness, everything that is limited and created is of no value and a bitter sorrow and pain. And so for him to be deprived of them is to be deprived of and freed from sorrow, affliction, and loss. To be deprived of sorrow is indeed a real consolation. For this reason, a man should not complain about loss. He ought to complain far more that he does not know consolation, that consolation cannot console him, just as sweet wine tastes sour to a sick man. He ought to complain, as I have written before, that he is not wholly free of creaturely images, and has not been transformed with all that he is into the image of the good.

A man in his sorrow ought also to remember that God speaks the truth and swears by himself, who is the Truth. If God were to fall short of his word, his Truth, he would fall short of his divinity and would not be God, for he is his word, his Truth. His word is that our sorrow will be turned into joy (Jn 16:20). Truly, if I knew for certain that every piece of stone that I had would be turned into gold, the more stones I possessed and the bigger they were, the gladder I should be; yes, I should go around begging for stones and collecting them, as big and as many as possible; and the more of them there were and the bigger, the happier they would make me. This surely would give a man mighty comfort in all his sorrow.

And there is another like this: No cask can hold two different kinds of drink. If it is to contain wine, then they must of necessity pour the water out; the cask must become empty and free. Therefore, if you are to receive God's joy and God, you are obliged to pour out created things. Saint Augustine says: "Empty yourself, so that you may be filled. Learn not to love, so that you may learn how to love. Draw back, so that you may be approached." In a few words: everything that is to receive and be capable of receiving should and must be empty. The authorities say that if the eye had some color in it when it was observing, it would recognize neither the color it had nor the color it had not, but because it is free of all colors, it therefore recognizes all colors. A wall has its own color, and therefore it recognizes neither its color nor any other color, and it takes no pleasure in colors, no more in that of gold or lapis lazuli than in that of charcoal. The eye has no color and yet truly possesses color, because it recognizes it with pleasure and delight and joy. And as the powers of the soul become more perfect and unmixed, so they apprehend more perfectly and comprehensively whatever they apprehend, receiving it more comprehensively, having greater joy, becoming more united with what they apprehend, to the point where the highest power of the soul, bare of all things and having nothing in common with anything, receives into itself nothing less than God himself, in all the vastness and fullness of his being. And the authorities show us that there is no delight and no joy that can be compared with this union and this fulfilling and this joy. This is why our Lord says so insistently: "Blessed are the poor in spirit" (Mt 5:3). A man is poor who has nothing. To be poor in spirit means that as the eye is poor and deprived of color, and is able to apprehend every color, so he is poor in spirit who is able to apprehend every spirit, and the Spirit of all spirits is God. The fruit of the spirit is love, joy, and peace (Gal 5:22). To be naked, to be poor, to have nothing, to be empty transforms nature; emptiness makes water flow uphill, and many other marvels of which we need not now speak.

Therefore, if you want to have and to find complete joy and consolation in God, make sure that you are naked of all created things, of all comfort from created things; for truly, as long as created things console you and can console you, never will you find true consolation. But when nothing but God can console you, then truly God does console you, and with him and in him everything that is joy consoles you. If what is not God consoles you, then you will have no consolation, neither now nor later. But if creatures do not console you and give you no delight, then you will find consolation, both now and to come.

If a man were able and knew how to make a goblet quite empty, and to keep it empty of everything that could fill it, even of air, doubtless the goblet would forgo and forget all its nature, and its emptiness would lift it up into the sky. And so to be naked, poor, empty of all created things lifts the soul up to God. Likeness and heat, too, draw up above. We attribute likeness in the divinity to the Son, heat and love to the Holy Spirit. Likeness in all things, but more so and first of all in the divine nature, is the birth of the One and the likeness of the One, in the One, and with the One; it is the beginning and the origin of flowering, fiery love. The One is the beginning without any beginning. Likeness is the beginning of the One alone, and it receives that it is and that it is beginning from the One and in the One. It is the nature of love that it flows and springs up out of two as one. One as one does not produce love, two as two does not produce love; two as one perforce produces natural, consenting, fiery love.

Solomon says that all waters—that is, all created things—flow and run back to their beginning (Ec 1:7). That is why what I have said is necessarily true. Likeness and fiery love draw up the soul and lead it and bring it to the first source of the One, which is "the Father of all," "in heaven and earth" (Eph 4:6, 3:15). And so I say that likeness, born of the One, draws the soul into God, as he is one in his hidden union, for that is what "One" signifies. Of this we have a plain example: When material fire kindles wood, a spark receives the nature of fire, and it becomes like pure fire, and without any medium sticks to the lower heavens. At once it forgets and denies father and mother, brother and sister down upon earth, and hastens up to the heavenly father. The father of the spark down here is the fire, and its mother is the wood, its brothers and sisters are the other sparks; but the first small spark does not wait for them. Swiftly it hastens up to its true father, which is the heavens; for anyone who recognizes truth knows very well that the fire is not the real true father of the spark, once it is fire. The real true father of the spark and of all fiery things is the heavens. And it should also be carefully observed that this little spark not only forsakes and forgets father and mother, brother and sister here upon earth; it forsakes and forgets and denies its own self out of its love to come to its lawful father, the heavens, because it must perforce be extinguished in the coldness of the air; and yet it wants to show its natural love, which it has for its true, heavenly father.

And as it has already been said about emptiness or nakedness, as the soul becomes more pure and bare and poor, and possesses less of created things, and is emptier of all things that are not God, it receives God more purely, and is more totally in him, and it truly becomes one with God, and it looks into God and God into it, face-to-face, as it were—two images transformed into one. This is what Saint Paul says, and this is what I say now about likeness and about the heat of love; because as one thing becomes more like another, so it hastens always faster toward it, and travels with greater speed, and its course is sweeter and more joyful to it. And the farther it goes away from itself and from everything that is not the object of its pursuit, the less like it becomes to itself and to everything that is not that object, and the more it becomes like the object toward which it drives. And because likeness flows from the One and draws and attracts by the power and in the power of the One, this does not pacify or satisfy that which is drawing or that which is being drawn, until they become united into one. Therefore the Lord said through the prophet Isaiah and meant that "no likeness, however exalted, and no loving peace will satisfy me, until I shine out myself in my Son" (Is 62:1), and until I myself am set on fire and enkindled in the love of the Holy Spirit. And our Lord prayed to his Father that we might become one with him and in him (Jn 17:11), not merely that we should be joined together. Of what this says, and of its truth, we have a plain example and proof even in the external natural order: When fire works, and kindles wood and sets it on fire, the fire diminishes the wood and makes it unlike itself, taking away its coarseness, coldness, heaviness, and dampness, and turns the wood into itself, into fire, more and more like to it. But neither the fire nor the wood is pacified or quieted or satisfied with any warmth or heat or likeness until the fire gives birth to itself in the wood, and gives to the wood its own nature and also its own being, so that they both become one and the same unseparated fire, neither less nor more. And therefore, before this may be achieved, there is always smoke, contention, crackling, effort, and violence between fire and wood. But when all the unlikeness has been taken away and rejected, then the fire is stilled and the wood is quiet. And I say something else that is true—that nature's hidden power secretly hates likeness insofar as it carries within itself distinction and duality, and nature seeks in likeness the One it loves for its own sake alone in likeness. So the mouth seeks and loves in the wine and from the wine its flavor or its sweetness. If water had the flavor that wine has, the mouth would love the wine no more than the water.

And that is why I have said that the soul hates likeness in likeness and does not love it in itself and for its own sake, but it loves likeness for the sake of the One that is concealed in likeness and is the true "Father," beginning without beginning, "of all in heaven and on earth" (Eph 4:6, 3:15). And therefore I say: as long as likeness can still be perceived and appears between fire and wood, there is never true delight or silence or rest or contentment. That is why the authorities say: fire comes about in strife and contention and unrest, and it happens in time; but the birth of the fire and joy is timeless, placeless. It seems to no one that delight and joy are slow or distant. Everything I have now said is signified when our Lord says: "When a woman gives birth to a child she has pain and anguish and sorrow; but when the child is born, she forgets the pain and anguish" (Jn 16:21). Therefore, too, God says in the Gospel and admonishes us that we should pray to the heavenly Father that our joy may be complete (Jn 15:11); and Saint Philip said: "Lord, show us the Father, and it is enough for us" (Jn 14:8). For "Father" implies birth, not likeness, and it signifies the One in which all likeness is stilled and everything is silenced that longs for being.

Now, a man may plainly see why and because of what he is unconsoled in all his sorrow, distress, and hurt. This all comes from nothing other than that he is far away from God, that he is not emptied of created things, that he is unlike to God, cold toward divine love.

Yet there is another matter; and anyone who would observe it and see it for what it is would soon be consoled in any worldly hurt and sorrow. Suppose that a man goes on a journey or undertakes some action or stops something else he is doing, and he suffers an injury. He breaks a leg, an arm, or loses an eye, or becomes sick. If then he keeps on thinking: "If you had taken another road, or if you had done something different, that would not have happened to you," he will remain unconsoled, and he is of necessity unhappy. That is why he should think: "If you had taken another road, or if you had started or stopped doing something different, some much worse injury or harm could easily have happened to you." And so he would rightly be consoled.

And I will put another case: If you have lost a thousand marks, you ought not to lament the thousand marks that are lost. You should thank God who gave you a thousand marks to lose, and who permits you to exercise the virtue of patience and so to gain that eternal life that many thousands of men will not possess.

Here is something else that can console a man. I put the case of someone who has enjoyed honors and ease for many years, and now loses them through God's decree. Then he should reflect wisely and thank God. When he feels his present harm and hurt, he realizes for the first time the profit and ease he used to have.

He should thank God for the ease he enjoyed for so many years and never acknowledged truly, when he was so well off, and he should not complain. He ought to reflect that a man of his own true nature has nothing of his own except sinfulness and weakness. Everything that is good and is goodness God has loaned him, not given him. Anyone who sees the truth knows that God, the heavenly Father, gives everything that is good to the Son and to the Holy Spirit. But to his creatures he gives nothing good; he lets them have it as a loan. The sun gives heat to the air, but makes a loan of light; and that is why as soon as the sun goes down, the air loses the light but the heat remains there—because the heat is given to the air to possess as its own. And that is why the authorities say that God, the heavenly Father, is Father and not Lord of the Son, nor is he the Lord of the Holy Spirit. But God, Father, Son, and Holy Spirit—this is one Lord, and the Lord of created things. We say that God was everlastingly the Father; but in time, in which he made created things, he is the Lord.

Now, I say: Since it is so, that everything that is good or comforting or temporal is only loaned to man, what cause has he to complain when he who has loaned it to him wishes to take it back? He ought to thank God, who has loaned it to him for so long. And he ought also to thank him that he does not take back everything he has loaned to him, as he well might take all his loan back, when the man becomes enraged because God takes from him a part of what was never his and of which he was never the owner. And that is why Jeremiah the prophet truly says of when he was in great sorrow and distress: "Many are the mercies of the Lord, that we are not wholly consumed" (Lam 3:22). If anyone had loaned me his coat and jerkin and cloak, and were to take back his cloak and leave me the coat and the jerkin against the cold, I ought to thank him greatly and be glad. And one ought to see clearly how very unjust I am if I storm and complain if I lose something; because if what I want is for the possessions I have to be given to me and not loaned, that means that I want to be Lord, and God's Son by nature—I who am not yet even God's son by grace—for it is the property of the Son of God and of the Holy Spirit to be unchanging in all circumstances.

One ought also to know that beyond any doubt even natural, human virtue is so excellent and so strong that there is no external work too difficult for it or great enough for it to manifest itself in it and through it and to form itself in it. And there is an interior work, which cannot be confined or comprehended by time or place; and in this work is what is divine and like to God, whom neither time nor place confine, for he is everywhere and present in all time, and this work is also like to God in this—that no creature can perfectly receive him nor form God's goodness in himself. And so there must be something more inward, more exalted, uncreated, lacking all measure, lacking all manner, in which the heavenly Father can form and pour and manifest his whole self; and that is the Son and the Holy Spirit. And no one can hinder this interior working of virtue, any more than anyone can hinder God. The work gleams and shines day and night. It lauds and sings God's praise and a new song; as David says: "Sing to God a new song" (Ps 95:1). God does not love that work whose praise is of the earth, for it is external, it is confined by time and place, it is narrow, men can hinder and force it, and it grows weary and old through time and labor. This work is to love God, to want good and goodness, and in this all that man wants and would do with a pure and perfect will in all good works has already been done, and in this he is like God, of whom David writes: "Whatever he pleased, he has already done and made" (Ps 134:6).

Of this teaching we have a clear example in stones, the external function of which is to fall down and to lie on the ground. This function can be prevented, and a stone does not keep on falling all the time. There is another function, more essential to the stone, and that is its propensity to fall, and that was made with it; neither God nor his creatures can take that away. The stone fulfills that function unceasingly, day and night. It can lie on the ground for a thousand years, but it will have the same propensity, neither less nor more, as on the first day.

This is what I mean when I say that virtue has an interior work: to want and to incline to everything that is good, to flee and oppose everything that is corrupt and evil and unlike goodness and God. And the worse that a deed is and the more unlike God, the greater is the opposition; and the greater a deed and the more like to God, the easier and more willing and joyful virtue finds it. And all its lament and sorrow, if sorrow could find any place in virtue, is that what is suffered for God is too little, and that all external works performed in time are too little, so that in them virtue cannot wholly show itself or fully manifest itself or form itself in them. Exercising itself, virtue grows strong, and in its generosity it becomes mighty. It would not wish to have finished suffering or to have vanquished sorrow and pain. It wishes and would always want unceasingly to continue suffering for the love of God and of doing good. All its blessedness is in suffering now, not in having suffered, for the love of God. And therefore our Lord says very plainly: "Blessed are they who suffer for the sake of justice" (Mt 5:10). He does not say "who have suffered." Such a man hates "having-suffered," for having-suffered is not the suffering he loves; it is a release from and a loss of suffering that he alone loves for the sake of God. And therefore I say that such a man also hates "shall-suffer," for that also is not suffering. But he hates shall-suffer less than he hates having-suffered, because having-suffered is further away from suffering and more unlike it, because it is wholly finished. If a man is yet to suffer, that does not entirely deprive him of the suffering he loves.

Saint Paul says that he would be willing to be deprived of God, for God's sake, so that God's glory might be increased (Rom 9:3). They say that Saint Paul said this at the time when he was not yet perfect; but I think that this saying came from a heart that was perfect. They say, too, that he meant that he wanted to be deprived of God for a time; but I say that a perfect man would be as loath to be deprived of God for one hour as for a thousand years. Yet if it was the will of God and to God's glory for him to be deprived of God, that would be as easy for him for a thousand years or for all eternity as for a day or an hour.

And the interior work is divine and of God and tastes of divinity in the sense that, just as all created beings, even if there were a thousand worlds, are not one hair's breadth better than is God alone, so I say now as I have said before that this external work does not at all add, not in its quantity or size or length or breadth, to the goodness of the interior work, which possesses its goodness in itself. Thus the external work can never be trivial if the interior work is great, and the external work can never be great or good if the interior work is trivial or worthless. The interior work contains in itself all time, all vastness, all breadth, and all length. The interior work receives and creates its whole being out of nowhere else than from and in the heart of God. It receives the Son, and is born Son in the bosom of the heavenly Father.

It is not so with the external work, for it has its divine goodness brought and poured into it by means of the interior work, as the divine nature stoops and clothes itself in distinction, in quantity, in division—all of which, and everything like it, and likeness itself, are far from God and alien to him. They seize upon and are seized and silenced by that which is good, enlightened, creaturely. They are wholly blind to what is in itself the good and the light, and to the One in which God brings to birth his Only Begotten Son, and to all who are God's children, his begotten sons. Here is the flowing out and the springing up of the Holy Spirit, from whom alone, as he is God's Spirit and himself Spirit, God the Son is conceived in us. Here is the flowing out of all those who are the sons of God, to the measure, greater or less, in which they are purely born of God alone, formed in God's likeness and in God, and strangers to all multiplicity, even though one does find multiplicity in the highest angels by their nature. And if we will see things truly, they are strangers to goodness, truth, and everything that tolerates any distinction, be it in a thought or in a name, in a notion or just a shadow of a distinction. They are intimates of the One that is bare of every kind of multiplicity and distinction. In the One, "God-Father-Son-and-Holy Spirit" are stripped of every distinction and property, and are one. And the One makes us blessed, and the farther we are away from the One, the less we are sons and the Son, and the less perfectly does the Holy Spirit spring up in us and flow out from us. And the closer we are to the One, the more truly are we God's sons and his Son, and also the more truly does God the Holy Spirit flow from us. This is what our Lord, God's Son in the divinity, means when he says: "Whoever drinks from the water that I shall give, in him will spring a fountain of water, springing up into life everlasting" (Jn 4:14). And Saint John says that he said that referring to the Holy Spirit (Jn 7:39).

The Son in the divinity according to his proper attribute gives nothing other than being son, nothing other than being born of God, source, the springing up and flowing out of the Holy Spirit, the love of God, nothing other than the full, true, and complete tasting of the One, of the heavenly Father. Therefore the Father's voice said from heaven to the Son: "You are my beloved Son, in whom I am loved and am well pleased" (Mt 3:17). For beyond doubt, no one loves God sufficiently and purely who is not God's son. For love, the Holy Spirit, springs and flows from the Son, and the Son loves the Father for the Father's sake, and loves the Father in himself, and loves himself in the Father. And therefore indeed

our Lord says that "the poor in spirit are blessed" (Mt 5:13)—
that is, those who have nothing of their own and of human spirit,
and who come naked to God. And Saint Paul says: "God has
manifested it to us in his Spirit" (Col 1:8).

Saint Augustine says that that man understands the scriptures
best of all who is free of all intellectual ambition and seeks only
for the sense and truth of the scriptures in scripture itself—
that is, in the Spirit, in whom the scriptures were written and
uttered, in the Spirit of God. Saint Peter says that all holy men
have spoken in the Spirit of God (2 Pt 1:21). Saint Paul says: "No
man knows what things may be in a man but the Spirit that is in
him, and no man can know what is the Spirit of God and is in
God except the Spirit, who is of God and is God" (1 Cor 2:11).

Therefore one commentary, a gloss, says very truly that no one
can understand or teach Saint Paul's writings if he does not possess
the Spirit in which Saint Paul spoke and wrote. And this is what I
always complain about: that crude men, empty of the Spirit of
God and not possessing it, want to judge according to their crude
human understanding what they hear or read in holy scripture,
which was spoken and written by and in the Holy Spirit, and that
they forget what is written—that what is impossible to man is
possible to God (Mt 19:26). That is also true in common things
and in the natural order: what is impossible to our lower nature is
commonplace and natural to our higher nature.

Understand, too, what I have just said—that a good man, a
son of God born in God, loves God for himself and in himself—
and much else that I have already said. To understand it better

one should know, as I have also often said, that a good man, born of goodness and in God, enters into all the attributes of the divine nature. Now, it is one attribute of God, according to the words of Solomon, that he forms all things for his own sake (Prv 16:4)—that is, that he does not look around outside himself for any reason other than himself; he loves and performs all things for his own sake. Therefore, if a man loves him and all things and performs all his works not for reward or honor or ease, but for God's sake and for his glory alone, that is a sign that he is God's Son.

What is more: God loves for his own sake and performs all things for his own sake; that is, he loves for love, and he works for working's sake. For without doubt, God would never have begotten in eternity his Only Begotten Son were not having begotten the same as begetting. That is why the saints say that as the Son was eternally begotten, so is he still being begotten without ceasing. Nor would God ever have created the world were not having been created the same as creating. Therefore God so created the world that he still without ceasing creates it. Everything that is past and that is yet to come is unknown to God and remote from him. And therefore whoever, born of God, is God's son loves God for his sake alone; that is, he loves God for the sake of loving God, and performs all his works for the sake of working. God never wearies of loving and working, and everything he loves is to him one love. And therefore it is true that God is love (1 Jn 4:16). And that is why I said before that a good man wants and would always want to suffer for God's sake, not to have suffered; for, suffering, he has what he loves. He loves suffering for God's sake, and he suffers for the sake of God. Therefore and thereby is he God's son, formed in God's likeness and in God, who loves for his own sake. That is, he loves for love, works for working; and therefore God loves and works without ceasing. And God's working is his nature, his being, his life, his blessedness. So truly, for God's son, a good man, inasmuch as he is God's son, to suffer and to work for the love of God is his being, his life, his working, his blessedness; for so our Lord says: "Blessed are they who suffer for justice's sake" (Mt 5:10).

Furthermore, I make a third point: A good man, insofar as he is good, has God's attributes not only in that he loves and works everything that he loves and works for the sake of God, whom he loves in everything and for love of whom he works, but he also loves and works for the sake of himself, who is the one loving. For what he loves, that is God, Father, Unbegotten; and he who loves is God, Son, Begotten. Now, the Father is in the Son, and the Son is in the Father (Jn 17:21). Father and Son are one. Seek at the end of this book for how the innermost and the highest part of the soul creates and receives God's Son and becoming-God's-Son in the bosom and heart of the heavenly Father, in what I write about "the nobleman who traveled far into a distant land to accept a kingdom and to return" (Lk 19:12).

One ought also to know that in nature, the impression and the influence of the highest and most exalted nature upon every man is to him more joyful and delightful than his self's own nature and being. By its own nature, water flows downhill, and in its flowing downhill is its being. But by the impression and the influence of the moon up above in the heavens, it denies and forgets its own nature and flows uphill, and to flow uphill is much easier for it than flowing downhill. Through this a man ought to know whether it is proper that he should delight and rejoice in wholly abandoning and denying his own natural will and in completely forsaking himself in everything God wants him to suffer. This is the best understanding of what our Lord said: "If any man will come to me, he should forsake and deny himself and take up his cross" (Mt 16:24)—that is, he should lay down and put away everything that is a cross and suffering. For truly, if anyone had denied himself and had wholly forsaken himself, nothing could be for him a cross or sorrow or suffering; it would all be a delight to him, a happiness, a joy to his heart, and he would truly be coming to God and following him. For just as nothing can grieve or afflict God, so nothing can make such a man rueful or sad. And therefore when our Lord says: "If any man will come to me, he should deny himself and take up his cross and follow me," it is not merely a command, as people usually say and think. It is a promise and a divine teaching about how all a man's suffering, all his work, all his life can become joyful and happy for him, and it is more a reward than a command. For such a man has everything he wants, and he wants nothing that is wrong; and that is blessedness. And that is indeed why our Lord says: "Blessed are they who suffer for the sake of justice" (Mt 5:10).

Furthermore, when our Lord, the Son, says: "Let him deny himself and lift up his cross and come to me," that means: let him become a Son, as I am Son, God-begotten, and let him become that same one that I am, which I, being and remaining in the bosom and the heart of the Father, create. "Father," the Son also says, "I wish the man who follows me, who comes to me, to be where I am" (Jn 12:26). No one truly comes to the Son as he is Son except the one who becomes son, and no one is where the Son is, who is one in the One in the Father's bosom and heart, except him who is son.

The Father says: "I will lead her into the wilderness and there speak to her heart" (Hos 2:14). Heart to heart, one in the One, so God loves. Everything that is alien to the One and far from it God hates. God invites and draws to the One. All creatures seek the One, the very meanest of created things seek the One, and the highest creatures find the One; drawn above their natures and transformed, they seek the One in the One, the One in its self. Perhaps this is why the Son says: "In the Son of divinity in the Father, where I am, he shall be who serves me, who follows me, who comes to me."

But there is yet another consolation. One ought to know that it is impossible to the whole of nature for it to break, spoil, or even touch anything in which it does not intend something better for the thing it touches. It is not enough for it to make something just as good; always it wants to make something better. How? A wise physician never touches a man's ailing finger so as to hurt the man if he cannot produce an improvement in the finger itself or in the whole man, and do him good. If he can cure the man and the finger, too, he does so; if he cannot, he amputates the finger to cure the man. And it is much better to lose the finger and to save the man than to lose both finger and man. One hurt is better than two, especially when one would be much greater than the other. One ought also to know that the finger and the hand and every member are naturally more concerned for the man to whom they belong than they are for themselves, and will gladly and unhesitatingly accept hardship and injury for the man's sake. I say with certainty and truth that the member does not love itself at all except insofar as it is a member. Therefore it would be very proper and would by nature be right for us not to love ourselves at all except for God's sake and in God. And if that were so, everything God wanted from us and in us would be easy and joyful for us, especially if we were convinced that God could not so easily allow our loss or harm if he did not know and intend that it would bring us a much greater benefit. Truly it is only too right for a man to suffer and be sad if he does not trust God.

There is another consolation. Saint Paul says that God chastises all those whom he receives and accepts as sons (Heb 12:6). It is part of our being a son for us to suffer. Because God's Son could not suffer in his divinity and in eternity, the heavenly Father therefore sent him into time, to become man and to be able to suffer. So if you want to be son of God and you do not want to suffer, you are all wrong. In the book of Wisdom it is written that God tests and tries whether a man is just, as men test and try gold and melt it in a furnace (Ws 3:5–6). It is a sign that the king or a prince has great trust in a knight when he sends him into battle. I knew a lord who, when he had accepted a knight into his service, would send him out by night and charge at him and fight with him. And once it happened that he was nearly killed by a man whom he wanted to test in this way, and he was much fonder of this soldier afterward than he had ever been.

We read that Saint Anthony in the desert was once in particular torment from evil spirits, and when he had overcome his distress our Lord appeared joyfully to him in bodily form. Then the holy man said: "O dear Lord, wherever were you when I was in such need?" Then our Lord said: "I was here, just where I am now; but it was my will and my pleasure to see how valiant you might be." A piece of silver or gold may be quite pure; but if they want to make a vessel out of it for the king to drink from, they will melt it down more thoroughly than another. That is why it is written of the apostles that they rejoiced that they were worthy to suffer contempt for the love of God (Acts 5:41).

God's Son by nature wanted to become man as a favor, so that he could suffer for your sake; and you want to become God's son and not man so that you cannot and need not suffer, either for love of God or of yourself.

Then, too, if a man knew and would consider what great joy, truly, God himself in his fashion, and all the angels and all who know and love God, have in the patience of the man who for God's sake suffers sorrow and harm—indeed through that alone he should rightly be comforted. For a man sacrifices his possessions and suffers harm so that he can bring joy to his friend and show some love for him.

And one might also think: if a man had a friend who for his sake was suffering and in sorrow and distress, it would certainly be the right thing to be with him and console him with his presence and with the consolations he could bring him. Of this the Lord says in the Psalms that he is with a good man in his sufferings (Ps 33:19). From these words one can draw seven teachings and a sevenfold consolation.

First, Saint Augustine says that patience in suffering for God's sake is better, dearer, higher, nobler than everything men can take away from a man against his will; for that is only his external possessions. God knows, one does not find anyone who loves this world who is so rich that he would not willingly and gladly suffer even for a long time great sorrow and pains if afterward he might be the mighty lord of all this world.

Second, I do not deduce from what God says merely that he is with man in his sufferings; but from what he says and in its spirit I deduce and say this: If God is with me in my suffering, what more or what else do I want? If I think rightly, I want nothing else and I want nothing more than God. Saint Augustine says: "He is too greedy and foolish who is not satisfied with God"; and elsewhere he says: "How can God's gifts, material or spiritual, satisfy the man who is not satisfied with God's own self?" And that is why he says in another place: "Lord, if you send us away from you, then give us another you, because we want nothing other than you." This is why the book of Wisdom says: "All good things come to me together with God, eternal Wisdom" (Ws 7:11). In one sense that means that nothing is good or can be good that comes without God, and everything that comes with God is good, and good only because it comes with God. About God I will not speak; but if one were to take away from all the creatures of this whole world the being God gives, they would remain a mere nothing, displeasing, worthless, and hateful. This saying contains much else of most excellent meaning about how all good things come with God, but it would take too long to talk about it now.

The Lord says: "I am with a man in suffering" (Ps 90:15). About this Saint Bernard says: "Lord, if you are with us in suffering, give me suffering always, so that you are always with me, so that I always have you."

Third, I say: that God is with us in suffering means that he himself suffers with us. Indeed, anyone who sees the truth knows that what I say is true. God suffers with man, he truly does; he suffers in his own fashion, sooner and far more than the man suffers who suffers for love of him. Now, I say: if God himself is willing to suffer, then I ought fittingly to suffer, for if I think rightly, I want what God wants. I pray every day as God commands me to pray: "Lord, may your will be done," and yet, if God's will is for suffering, I want to complain about suffering; and that is not right at all. And I say, too, with certainty, that since God suffers so willingly with us and for our sake, if we suffer only for love of him, he suffers without suffering. Suffering is for him so joyful that it is for him not suffering. And therefore, if we thought rightly, suffering would not be suffering for us; it would be our joy and consolation.

Fourth, I say that a friend's compassion naturally makes this suffering less. If then the compassion that a man has for me can console me, God's compassion should console me far more.

Fifth, if I should suffer with a man whom I loved and who loved me, and I wanted this, then I ought gladly and fittingly to suffer with God, who is suffering in this with me and suffers for my sake, out of the love that he has for me.

Sixth, I say that if God has suffered already, before ever I suffer, and if I suffer for the love of God, truly all my sufferings will easily turn into my consolation and joy, however great and varied my suffering may be. This is true in the natural order: If a man does something for something else's sake, that for the sake of which he does it is closer to his heart, and what he does is further from his heart, and only touches his heart through that which is the object and cause of what he does. If someone is building, hewing wood and breaking stone, with the intention of making a house as a shelter against the summer's heat and the winter's frost, his heart is set, chiefly and wholly, on the house; he is not cutting the stone or doing the labor except for the sake of the house. We see well that if a sick man drinks sweet wine, it seems to him bitter and he says that it is; and this is true, because the wine loses all its sweetness outside, on the bitterness of the tongue, before it can penetrate to where the soul recognizes and judges its flavor. This is so, far more and more truly, of a man who performs all his works for the love of God. Then God is the medium, and he is what is closest to the soul. Nothing can touch a man's heart and soul that for God's sake and through his sweetness does not lose and must lose its bitterness and become wholly sweet before it can ever touch a man's heart.

There is another token and simile that signifies this. The authorities say that beneath the heaven there is a vast extent of fire, and that therefore no rain or wind or any kind of storm or tempest from below can reach so close to the heaven that anything can touch it; everything is burned up and consumed by the fire's heat before it can reach heaven. So I say that everything a man suffers and performs for God's sake becomes wholly sweet in God's sweetness before it can reach the heart of the man who works and suffers for the love of God. That is what we mean when we say "for the love of God," for nothing can ever come to the heart except by flowing through God's sweetness, in which it loses its bitterness. And it is also consumed in the fiery heat of the divine love, which has wholly enclosed the good man's heart.

Now, one can plainly see how fittingly and variously a good man is comforted on all sides in suffering, in sorrow, and in working. One way is for him to suffer and work for the love of God; another way is for him to be in the divine love. And a man can see and know whether he performs all his works for the love of God and whether he is in God's love. For when a man finds himself sorrowful and unconsoled, to that extent his work was not done for God alone, and you may be sure that to that extent he is not wholly in God's love. King David says that a fire comes with God and before him, consuming everything God finds opposed to him and unlike him (Ps 96:3)—that is, sorrow, despair, strife, and bitterness.

And the seventh teaching from the saying that God is with us in suffering and suffers with us is that we should be mightily comforted by God's attribute—that he is the purely one, without any accidental admixture of distinction, even in thought; that everything that is in him is God himself. And because that is true, therefore I say: everything the good man suffers for God's sake, he suffers in God, and God is suffering with him in his suffering. But if my suffering is in God and God is suffering with me, how then can suffering be sorrow to me, if suffering loses its sorrow, and my sorrow is in God, and my sorrow is God? Truly, as God is Truth and as I find the Truth, I find my God, the Truth, there; and, too, neither less nor more, as I find pure suffering for the love of God and in God, I find God my suffering. If anyone does not recognize this, let him blame his blindness, not me, and not God's truth and loving generosity.

So suffer in this way for God's sake, since this is so greatly profitable and brings such blessedness. "Blessed are they," our Lord said, "who suffer for the sake of justice" (Mt 5:10). How can God, who loves goodness, suffer his friends, who are good men, not to be in suffering always and without ceasing? If a man had a friend who could, by suffering for a few days, so earn great profit and honor and ease and possess it for a long time, and he wanted to hinder that or let it be hindered by anyone else, no one would say that he could be the other man's friend or that he loved him. Therefore, far less could God suffer in any way that his friends, good men, should ever be without suffering, unless they were able to suffer without suffering. Any good in external suffering proceeds and flows from the goodness of the will, as I have already written. And therefore everything a good man wished and is ready and longs to suffer for God's sake he suffers in God's sight and, for God's sake, in God. King David says in the Psalms: "I am ready for every hardship, and my suffering is continually before me" (Ps 37:18)—in my heart and in my sight. Saint

Jerome says that a piece of pure wax, quite pliable and serviceable to have this or that made out of it according to someone's intention and wish, contains within it everything anyone can make with it, even though no one actually makes anything from it. And I have written before that the stone does not weigh any less if one cannot see it lying on the ground; all its weight is completely present because it is in itself capable of falling and ready to fall. And I have also written already that the good man has already performed in heaven and on earth everything he wished to do, and in this, too, he is like God.

Now, one can see and know how stupid the people are who are always surprised when they see good men suffering pain and harm; and often in their folly they wrongly imagine that this must be for such men's secret sins. And then sometimes they say: "Oh, I thought he was a very good man! How can it be that he is suffering such great sorrow and harm, when I thought that he was perfect?" And I agree with them: certainly, if this were suffering, and if they did suffer sorrow and misfortune, then they would not be good or free from sin. But if they are good, then suffering for them is not sorrow or misfortune, but it is their great good fortune and blessedness. "Blessed," said God, who is Truth, "are all those who suffer for the sake of righteousness." Therefore the book of Wisdom says: "The souls of the just are in the hand of God. The unwise think and imagine that they die and perish, but they are in peace" (Ws 3:1)—in joy and blessedness. When Saint Paul writes of how many of the saints have suffered so many great torments, he says that the world was not worthy of

this (Heb 11:36–38); and for anyone who understands this saying, it has a threefold meaning. One is that this world is not worthy that many good men live in it. Another and better meaning
tells us that what counts as goodness in the world is base and
worthless; God alone has worth, and therefore they are worthy
before God and of God. The third meaning, which is the one I
now have in mind and wish to state, is that this world—that is,
the people who love this world—are not worthy to suffer sorrow
and hardship for God's sake. Of this it is written that the holy
apostles rejoiced that they were worthy to suffer torment for the
name of God (Acts 5:41).

Let what I have said now be enough, because in the third part
of this book I want to write of various consolations with which a
good man can and should comfort himself in his sorrow, and
which one can find not only in the words but also in the deeds of
good and wise men.

Part 3

We read in the book of Kings that a man cursed King David and
said what was deeply shameful to him (2 Kgs 16:5). Then one of
David's friends said that he would strike this vile dog dead. But
the king said: "No! because perhaps it is God's will through this
shame to do what is best for me."

We read in the Lives of the Fathers that a man complained to a holy
father that he was suffering. Then the father said: "My son, do you
want me to pray to God to take it away from you?" Then the

other said: "No, father, because it is profitable to me—that I see well. But pray to God to give me his grace so that I suffer it willingly."

Once someone asked a sick man why he did not pray to God to make him well. Then the man said that there were three reasons he would be sorry to do that. The first was that he wanted to be sure our loving God would never allow him to be sick, if that was not the best thing for him. The second reason was that if a man is good, he wants everything God wishes, and not that God should wish what he may want, for that would be wholly wrong. And therefore if it is his will that I should be sick—and if he did not will it so, it would not be so—then I ought not to wish to be well. For without any doubt, if it could be that God might make me well against his will, it would seem to me unworthy and base that he should make me well. Willing comes from loving, unwilling comes from unloving. It is dearer and better and more profitable to me that God should love me and that I should be sick than for me to be well in my body and for God not to love me. What God loves, that is something; but what God does not love, that is nothing, as the book of Wisdom says (Ws 11:25). And it is also true that everything God wills, in that and because God wills it, is good. Truly, to speak in ordinary language, I should rather that some rich and mighty man—a king, maybe—should love me and yet leave me for a while without any gift than that he should straightaway order me to be given something, and that he should not in fact love me. Let him now not give me anything because of his love, and yet not give me anything now because he wishes later to make me richer and greater gifts. And even if I suppose that the man who loves me and who gives me nothing now does not propose to give me anything later, perhaps he will think better of this afterward and will give me something. I ought to wait patiently, especially because his gift is gratuitous and unmerited. And certainly, if I do not esteem someone's love, and if my will is opposed to his will, unless I receive a gift from him, it is very right that he give me nothing, and that he hate me and leave me as wretched as I am.

The third reason it would not be of value and of importance to me to want to ask God to make me well is that I do not wish to and I should not ask our mighty, loving, merciful God for so small a thing. If I were to go a hundred or two hundred miles to see the pope, and I were to come into his presence and say: "Lord, holy father, I have come all of two hundred miles, a hard journey that has cost a lot, and I ask Your Holiness, because this is what I have come for, to give me a bean," truly, he and anyone else who heard it would say, and rightly, that I was a perfect idiot. Now, what I say is gospel truth: all possessions and indeed all created things are in comparison with God less than is a bean in comparison with all this physical world. Therefore I should do well, if I was a good and wise man, to be ashamed of asking that I might get well.

On this topic I say, too, that it is the sign of a sick heart if a man becomes glad or sorry over the transitory things of this world. We should feel shame for this in our hearts in the sight of God and his angels, and in the sight of men, that we should detect this in

ourselves. We are ashamed soon enough of some facial disfigure-
ment that is there for people to see. What more do I need to say?
The books of the Old Testament and the New, and those of the
saints and even the pagans, are full of this: how pious men for
God's sake and also for the sake of natural virtue have given their
lives and have willingly sacrificed themselves.

A pagan philosopher, Socrates, says that virtue makes impossible things possible, and even easy and delightful. And I must
not forget that the blessed woman of whom the book of the
Maccabees tells that in a single day she saw enacted before her
own eyes the horrifying and horrible torments, intolerable
even to hear about, that were inflicted and imposed upon her
seven sons—that she watched this cheerfully and encouraged
and particularly admonished them not to be afraid, and to surrender willingly their bodies and their spirits for the sake of
God's justice.

This could be the end of the book, but there are two more
things that I want to say. The first thing is that truly a good and
pious man ought to be bitterly and greatly ashamed that suffering
ever moved him, when we see how a merchant, for the sake of
earning a little money—of which, too, he cannot be sure—will
travel so far overland on arduous tracks, up hill and down dale,
across wildernesses and oceans, risking robbery and assault on
his person and his goods, going in great want of food and drink
and sleep, and suffering other hardships, and yet he is glad and
willing to forget all this for the sake of his small and uncertain
profit. A knight in a battle risks possessions and body and life for

the sake of a transient and very fleeting honor; and yet we think it such a great matter that we should suffer a little for God's sake, who is everlasting blessedness.

The second thing is that I expect that many stupid people will say that much that I have written in this book and elsewhere is not true. To that I reply with what Saint Augustine says in the first book of his *Confessions*. He says that God has already made every single thing, everything that is still to come for thousands and thousands of years, if this world should last so long, and that everything that is past during many thousands of years he will make again today. Is it my fault if people do not understand this? And he says in another place that a man's self-love is too blatant when he wants to blind other men so that his own blindness may be hidden. It is enough for me that what I say and write be true in me and in God. If anyone sees a stick pushed down into the water, it seems to him that the stick is bent, although it is quite straight; and the reason for this is that water is cruder than air. But yet the stick is straight and not bent, both in itself and also in the eyes of anyone who looks at it only through the pure air.

Saint Augustine says: "Whoever without thought of any kind, or without any kind of bodily likeness and image, perceives within himself what no external vision has presented to him, — he knows that this is true." But the man who knows nothing of this will laugh at me and mock me, and I can only pity him. But people like this want to contemplate and taste eternal things and the works of God, and to stand in the light of eternity, and yet their hearts are still fluttering around in yesterday and tomorrow.

A pagan philosopher, Seneca, says: "We must speak about great and exalted matters with great and exalted understanding and with sublime souls." And we shall be told that one ought not to talk about or write such teachings to the untaught. But to this I say that if we are not to teach people who have not been taught, no one will ever be taught, and no one will ever be able to teach or write. For that is why we teach the untaught: so that they may be changed from uninstructed into instructed. If there was nothing new, nothing would ever grow old. Our Lord says: "Those who are healthy do not need medicine" (Lk 5:31). That is what the physician is there for: to make the sick healthy. But if there is someone who misunderstands what I say, what is that to the man who says truly that which is true? Saint John narrates his holy Gospel for all believers and also for all unbelievers, so that they might believe, and yet he begins that Gospel with the most exalted thoughts any man could utter here about God; and both what he says and what our Lord says are constantly misunderstood.

May our loving and merciful God, who is Truth, grant to me and to all those who will read this book that we may find the truth within ourselves and come to know it. Amen.

ABOUT THE EDITOR

HarperCollins Spiritual Classics Series Editor Emilie Griffin has long been interested in the classics of the devotional life. She has written a number of books on spiritual formation and transformation, including Clinging: The Experience of Prayer and Wilderness Time: A Guide to Spiritual Retreat. With Richard J. Foster she coedited Spiritual Classics: Selected Readings on the Twelve Spiritual Disciplines. Her latest book is Wonderful and Dark Is This Road: Discovering the Mystic Path. She is a board member of Renovaré and leads retreats and workshops throughout the United States. She and her husband, William, live in Alexandria, Louisiana.

ABOUT JOHN O'DONOHUE

John O'Donohue, writer of the Foreword, is an Irish poet and philosopher who is currently working on a post-doctoral dissertation on Meister Eckhart. His two collections of poetry are Echoes of Memory and Conamara Blues. He is the author of a book on the philosophy of Georg Wilhelm Friedrich Hegel, Person als Vermittlung. His three books on spirituality are Anam-Cara: Wisdom from the Celtic World; Eternal Echoes: Exploring Our Yearning to Belong; and Beauty: The Invisible Embrace. Also, for more on Eckhart, see O'Donohue's article in the Spring 2003 issue of The Eckhart Review, "The Absent Threshold: The Paradox of Divine Knowing in Meister Eckhart." For more about John O'Donohue visit www.jodonohue.com.

THE CLASSICS OF **WESTERN SPIRITUALITY**
A LIBRARY OF THE GREAT SPIRITUAL MASTERS

These volumes contain original writings of universally acknowledged teachers within the Catholic, Protestant, Eastern Orthodox, Jewish, Islamic, and American Indian traditions.

The Classics of Western Spirituality unquestionably provide the most in-depth, comprehensive, and accessible panorama of Western mysticism ever attempted. From the outset, the Classics has insisted on the highest standards for these volumes, including new translations from the original languages, and helpful introductions and other aids by internationally recognized scholars and religious thinkers, designed to help the modern reader to come to a better appreciation of these works that have nourished the three monotheistic faiths for centuries.

Bonaventure
Translated and Introduced by Ewert Cousins
0-8091-2121-2 $24.95

Teresa of Avila
Edited and Introduced by Kieran Kavanaugh, O.C.D.
0-8091-2254-5 $22.95

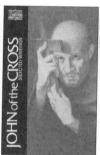
John of the Cross
Edited and Introduced by Kieran Kavanaugh, O.C.D.
0-8091-2839-X $21.95

Meister Eckhart
Translated and Introduced by Edmund College, O.S.A., and Bernard McGinn
0-8091-2370-3 $22.95

For more information on the
CLASSICS OF WESTERN SPIRITUALITY, contact Paulist Press
(800) 218-1903 • www.paulistpress.com